SURFING FOR ENGLAND OUR
LOST SOCCEROOS

SURFING FOR ENGLAND OUR LOST SOCCEROOS

Jason Goldsmith

First published in 2019 by Fair Play Publishing
PO Box 4101, Balgowlah Heights NSW 2093 Australia

www.fairplaypublishing.com.au
sales@fairplaypublishing.com.au

ISBN: 978-0-925914-00-9
ISBN: 978-0-925914-01-6 (ePUB)

© Jason Goldsmith 2019.
The moral rights of the author have been asserted.

All rights reserved. Except as permitted under the *Australian Copyright Act 1968* (for example, a fair dealing for the purposes of study, research, criticism or review), no part of this book may be reproduced, stored in a retrieval system, communicated or transmitted in any form or by any means without prior written permission from the Publisher.

Cover design and page layout by Leslie Priestley.

Photographs supplied by Adelaide Croatia FC, DT38, Andrew Durante, and Alamy.
Front cover: Craig Johnston playing for Liverpool in a FA Cup match, March 1987.
Back cover: Tony Dorigo pictured with his hand on the ball playing for England in the third-place play-off against Italy at World Cup Italia 90.

$1 from the sale of every copy of this book will be given by Fair Play Publishing to the DT38 Foundation.

All inquiries should be made to the Publisher via sales@fairplaypublishing.com.au

A catalogue record of this book is available from the National Library of Australia.

Contents

Foreword by Santo Cilauro		vii
Introduction		ix
1	Surfing for England – Craig Johnston	1
2	England's Colonials – Tony Dorigo	9
3	Acceptance and Excellence – Our Indigenous stars: Perkins, Briscoe, Moriarty	15
4	Green and Gold Goalkeeping Glut – Didulica and Ilic	23
5	Goals Gone Missing – Porta, Smeltz, Vieri	32
6	Australia's taxpayer funded stars – Seric, Ergic, Simunic	41
7	DT38 – Dylan Tombides	51
8	Righting the wrongs – The Cahill Rule	58
9	Chasing Higher Honours – The Aussies who went another way	65
10	Lost Socceroos Short Stories	75
Acknowledgements		82
About Jason Goldsmith		84

Foreword

I grew up feeling The Pain. Sometimes it was piercing, other times dull and numbing. Strangely enough, it was always exquisite. The Socceroos served it up in many different ways. Qualifying for World Cups was hard on everyone – players, coaches, administration and, of course, us, the loyal fans.

The epitaphs of lost campaigns all read, "Shoulda Coulda Woulda". Earnest conversations beginning with the words "If only…" or "What if…" still echo through the smoky pubs of the late seventies, eighties, nineties and first half of the (slightly less smoky) noughties.

Unlike any other account of our game, Jason Goldsmith's history of who *didn't* play for Australia as opposed to who *did* - is unique. He ushers us through a labyrinth of sliding doors into a parallel universe of whys and why nots that leaves us thinking not just about the shortcomings of the past but how to deal with the challenges of the future.

And fear not - if theories, conspiracies, football politics or sports psychology are not your cups of tea, *Surfing For England – Our Lost Socceroos* is, at its heart, a collection of ripping stories quintessentially Australian.

Santo Cilauro
Melbourne, Australia

Introduction

Selection is an opinion-based game and completely subjective across the world. Why do some players get picked for representative sides as opposed to others?

In the original Socceroos teams of the 1920s and 1930s, some teams needed to fill interstate quotas; some players get injured before their time and never get a chance to make rep sides; some players might be good enough but have two or three above them in the same position; some coaches pick players that have "done a job" for them at club level so get precedence.

Selection for any team, let alone the Socceroos, is not an exact science.

I realise this book could include anyone who has kicked a ball in Australia and I'm sure it will start debates about who should be included.

The focus has been on some of the best footballers in Australia who did not play for the national team.

The concept of Lost Socceroos shows us what outstanding football talent Australia has produced and who, for varying reasons, didn't allow them to pull on the green and gold of Australia.

Imagine John Moriarty and Charlie Perkins leading Australia into World Cup qualifying campaigns.

Imagine the 1985 Socceroos taking on Scotland in World Cup qualifying featuring English First Division players Craig Johnston and Tony Dorigo.

Imagine the 1997 Socceroos taking on Iran at the MCG and Christian Vieri makes the most of those first half opportunities scoring two or three early goals

Imagine in the 2006 World Cup Round of 16 Socceroo Joe Simunic tackles Italian Fabio Grosso, he wins the ball and both players keep their feet.

Imagine in the 2011 Asian Cup final against Japan, Shane Smeltz or Richard Porta breaking the deadlock up front or a young Dylan Tombides scoring the winner against Denmark in the 2018 World Cup.

Sadly these things never happened, and there were a variety of reasons we have lost Socceroos.

The tyranny of distance, lack of meaningful internationals, jeopardising club careers, tragic illnesses, no FIFA international windows, being in the Oceania zone, choosing the country of your heritage, being selected but FIFA banning Australia from internationals, not being considered despite form, choosing to chase higher honours with other countries, playing junior football in the old NSL system, being tapped on the shoulder by the country of your residence or courted by better footballing countries and systems. There are many and varied reasons why some of these footballers never played for Australia.

These players should be recognised as Australian talent who have played a part in our game's history and now will help to shape our game's future.

I hope to tell a small part about our lost Socceroos.

Jason Goldsmith
Melbourne, Australia

1
'Surfing for England' – Craig Johnston

"Playing soccer for Australia would be like surfing for England."

So said a young footballer on the popular national current affairs television show *60 Minutes* to reporter George Negus in 1981.

The footballer was from Newcastle, part of the historic Australian football region in the mid-coast of New South Wales, and he was in England playing in the top flight for Middlesbrough. The interview preceded him making a move to Liverpool, the biggest football club in the world at the time.

His name was Craig Johnston and he is one of the best footballers Australia has produced. Yet he never played for the Socceroos.

Johnston's father Colin was an established football player in the Newcastle region of Australia. As a young kid playing football, Johnston's father nicknamed him '*Reg*' after Socceroo and Newcastle football goal scoring legend, Reg Date. When Johnston got to the UK he was christened '*Roo*' by his teammates.

His journey to the UK was one of sheer determination and family sacrifice, and it all began with Johnston watching Middlesbrough on TV during their pre-season trip to Australia in 1975.

Fresh from winning the English second division in 1974-75, Middlesbrough played a Northern NSW representative team in Newcastle. In the papers the following day, there was a story about the English club offering local Aussie teenager Joe Senkalski a trial in the UK.

Although it didn't work out for Senkalski, it planted the seed for Johnston and his football ambitions. (Senkalski, by the way, became a Socceroo and played more than 200 national league games in Australia).

Johnston wrote to four clubs in England about potential trials: Chelsea, Manchester United, Fulham and Middlesbrough. Only Middlesbrough responded to the letter and the family decided that they would send the then 15-year old to the UK for this trial.

The big issue facing the Johnstons with this news would be the cost to the family. In the 1970s, funding a trip to the UK was expensive.

The Johnston's sold their family home and moved into a small cottage on the waterfront of Lake Macquarie at Fishing Point, south of Newcastle, saving enough money to fund the trip.

This sacrifice would be at the forefront of Johnston's mind throughout his career, never wanting to jeopardise what his parents and family had done to support his dream.

It was during these formative football years for Johnston at Middlesbrough, before he had established himself in the first team, that he needed some assistance in the off season. Johnston wanted to return to Australia to help him recover from a pelvis injury and also to see his grandmother who was gravely ill.

"It was the off season and all the Irish, Scottish and Welsh players that were at Middlesbrough as triallists, they all went home. So did the English kids. So I was the only kid left at Middlesbrough, on my own and I was also injured. I had a serious injury to my pelvis and I needed to go home to Australia but I couldn't afford to get there. So I phoned the Australian Soccer Federation and spoke to a guy called Alan Vessey and I said *'Look I'm injured, I can't afford the fare back home, and I'm here on my own now because all the other triallists had gone home.*"

Australian soccer didn't help Johnston, and in those days, there was no Professional Footballers Association to turn to.

Instead, the assistance came from the Middlesbrough manager, John Neal.

"The manager heard about it and he paid my fare."

On his return to the UK after his grandmother's passing and having recovered from the pelvis injury, things really started to pick up for Johnston.

After toiling away at Middlesbrough as an apprentice, through sheer will, determination, hard work and constant practice that included extra solo sessions, he made it as a professional footballer.

They progressed to the level that Johnston established himself as a star on the rise in the English first division, which then captured the attention of *60 Minutes* journalist George Negus.

Negus was brought up with soccer and had heard about a young kid from Newcastle, making waves in England.

"I spent the week with him in Middlesbrough, that's how we got to know each other," says Negus.

"It was in the off season for *60 Minutes*, I think I did the piece in late November but it did not go to air until February.

"He asked me what I wanted him to do when I was there and I said, '*score a bloody goal*' and he did. He scored a goal for me."

Prior to the *60 Minutes* episode going to air Johnston was attracting attention from the big clubs in the UK, with offers coming from Aston Villa, Leeds United, Manchester City, Arsenal, Tottenham, West Brom and Nottingham Forest.

It was Liverpool and Bob Paisley who made the best pitch, and after speaking with his father back in Australia for some advice, Craig Johnston was off to Anfield. Big games, trophies and recognition were all ahead of him with that move.

By the time Negus' story went to air, Johnston had become a Liverpool player.

Negus says he provoked Johnston somewhat to get the famous "*Surfing for England*" quote.

"I actually said to him that there are a lot of people back home who aren't terribly pleased at the idea that you haven't come back to play for your country," says Negus.

According to Johnston himself, it was an off the cuff remark from a 20-year old kid just trying to make it in the English first division.

"There were no FIFA windows and there was no procedure or protocol for anyone to get back to another country to play for that country.

"People forget all of this stuff and clearly it's handy for a journalist to quote the George Negus thing about surfing for England. But I loved Australia and I loved football, I still do.

"So the quote was kind of a sort of dumb, stupid young kid thing to say."

What Negus' story did achieve was to put Johnston back in front of Australian football officials. Not long after the story was aired, he was asked to play for Australia in the qualifying games for the 1982 World Cup.

"The Australian Soccer Federation phoned me and said we want you to play for Australia."

After the bitter episode of not being helped to get back to see his grandmother and recover from injury, playing for the Socceroos seemed a long shot. Johnston was not willing to jeopardise his place in the Liverpool team.

"I was over there punching away, trying to be the best player I could be and Australian soccer had abandoned me."

Australia did come calling again, four years later for the qualifying campaign for the 1986 World Cup.

Socceroos coach Frank Arok made an approach to Johnston when he was home in Newcastle in the off season. Arok wanted him for the away tie against Israel and, if successful, to be followed by the two home and away games against a European opponent (which turned out to be Sir Alex Ferguson's Scotland).

Johnston and Arok met in the Newcastle Rugby Club, so as to not arouse suspicion and to lessen the chances of recognition.

Following this meeting, Johnston and Arok agreed that they both required some clarification on whether Johnston was still eligible to play for the Socceroos given he had played two Under 21 games for England. However, Johnston wasn't 100%

committed to playing these three games for Australia, and he wanted permission from Liverpool to do so.

In Johnston's 1989 biography '*Walk Alone*'(co-written with Neal Jameson) he writes about the fallout from that meeting with Arok:

"Within a fortnight of that meeting a story declaring that I was ineligible to play for Australia appeared in a Sydney newspaper. It was sourced to an Australian Soccer Federation administrator who had said that the situation had been investigated by FIFA, the governing body of world football, and that Johnston was definitely out of contention."

Johnston called the Australian Soccer Federation to seek clarification on this stance and was told that he was not eligible for the Socceroos and that they had even spoken with English Football Association Secretary Ted Croker to check the ruling.

As luck would have it, Ted Croker shared a flight with Johnston from Japan, following on from the 1984 World Club Championships in Tokyo. Johnston approached him asking for some clarification on the ruling. Croker denied having spoken to the Australian Soccer Federation but promised to investigate the matter personally. Croker responded to Johnston via letter, part of which was also published in '*Walk Alone*'.

"Further to our discussion in Japan, I have now investigated the situation regarding your international appearances for our Under 21 team.

"I have a positive assurance now from FIFA that these matches will not in any way prejudice your eligibility to play for Australia, assuming that, as I believe you stated, you have an Australian passport and are a national of that country."

Johnston was so disheartened with the actions and attitude of the Australian football officials that he vowed he would never play for Australia.

According to friend and a younger Socceroos star of that era, Frank Farina, the players didn't consider Johnston would play for them, but didn't begrudge him at all. To do so, in their eyes, would have jeopardised his career in the UK.

"He would have been a great asset for us, he would have been a wonderful player to have in the national team in terms of just driving everyone on," Farina says.

"As players we used to talk about it sometimes - how good would it be if he came back. We weren't a big force, we were mostly playing club teams and minnow nations in Oceania."

Whilst the national team was playing against the likes of club sides such as Shamrock Rovers, Fortuna Sittard and IFK Göteborg, Johnston was playing at Anfield, Old Trafford, Goodison Park and Wembley.

A midfielder, Johnston was a standout in the mid 1980s for the Reds, most famous for scoring a goal in the 1986 FA Cup final against Everton in a 3-1 victory to Liverpool. It was one of the few games screened live on Australian television at the time.

His final game for Liverpool was in the 1988 FA Cup final, coming on in the 64th minute for Irishman John Aldridge. He couldn't help Liverpool as they went down 1-0 to Wimbledon in front of 98,203 fans at Wembley in what was a huge upset.

Johnston retired at the age of 28, in his prime and at the height of his career to return to Australia to be with his sister, Faye. She had been in an accident while holidaying in Morocco, and with a young family, Johnston believed he needed to be with them.

It was during this time that Johnston developed a range of other interests including broadcasting and photography among other things. He also developed the revolutionary football boot known as the '*Predator*'.

The Predator was designed with increased grip through rubber on the toe of the boot enabling the player to have more control with the ball. Initially rejected by Adidas, Nike and Reebok, Johnston eventually sold the design to Adidas, five years after developing the concept.

The successful sales pitch was footage of German football legend Franz Beckenbauer wearing the boots in snowy conditions.

In 1994 the first Adidas Predator boot was released, and in April that year John Collins of Celtic scored the first ever Predator goal, a free kick on the edge of the box in an Old Firm derby against Rangers at Ibrox Stadium in a 1-1 draw. It wouldn't be the last Predator goal. The boot was so successful it was worn and championed by the likes of David Beckham and Zinedine Zidane.

The Predator range was the first time Adidas chose a different colour scheme for their boots other than black, and since the original was released in 1994 there have been 21 new versions of this football boot.

Johnston still loved Australia and was always trying to assist the game here when he could, but he always seemed to be knocked back when he did.

By the 1990s George Negus had also joined the board of Soccer Australia and tried to get Johnston involved in the game in an official capacity.

"He came to Australia every time and tried to talk to administrations. He couldn't get anywhere with them, they weren't interested.

"Eddie Thompson went out of his way to be an arsehole to Craig, and I am surprised they never came to fisticuffs, I heard it was awful, calling him a sellout," Negus explains.

Negus said that with a new administration in place, including himself, Johnston was quite happy to try and get back involved.

"Because David Hill and I were involved and he knew we were cleanskins, and he knew that we were getting nothing out of it other than the love of the game itself."

In 1997 when Australia were heading into the World Cup qualification stage for the 1998 World Cup in France, Johnston reached out to his friend George Negus. Negus was living in Italy at the time and remembers it. Johnston has been unofficially sounding-out potential coaches for the Socceroos of the profile and calibre of Roy Hodgson.

"He rang me. The telephone reception in those days was pretty ordinary, so I went to the top of a hill in the Chianti district, drove up where I could get some service, spoke to Craig and he said *'If you blokes are serious I reckon we can get Terry Venables to coach the Socceroos'.*"

Terry Venables was a big name in English football. He played over 500 games with the likes of Chelsea, Tottenham and Queens Park Rangers as well as for England. As a manager he had coached Crystal Palace, Queens Park Rangers, Barcelona and Tottenham. At the time he had just taken England to the semi-finals of the 1996 European Championships, where they were defeated on penalties by the eventual champion's Germany. He had a massive profile.

History shows that the then Australian Soccer Federation Chairman David Hill and Board member, Basil Scarcella, went to England and convinced Venables to manage the Socceroos.

In November 1997, more than 95,000 people at the Melbourne Cricket Ground saw the Socceroos draw 2-2 with Iran and miss World Cup Qualification on the away goals rule after having drawn the first leg match 1-1 in Tehran.

The Socceroos side, which featured the likes of Mark Bosnich, Robbie Slater, Craig Foster, Steve Horvat, Aurelio Vidmar, Stan Lazaridis and Ned Zelic, went through the qualifying campaign undefeated but missed out at the final hurdle. Youngsters Mark Viduka and Harry Kewell would eventually get there in 2006 and, according to Negus, the short Venables coaching tenure paved the way for what was to come.

"It's true to say that Craig's contribution to Australian football was to give it a totally new future by getting a high-profile coach."

After another failed World Cup campaign for the 2002 tournament, Australia were able to appoint their next big name in world football when Dutchman Guus Hiddink took them to Germany in 2006.

Despite varying football and business interests, Johnston was always willing to help out Australian football people following his playing career.

When Frank Farina was coach, Johnston would do special coaching sessions with the Socceroos.

Bonita Mersiades has had a long association with Johnston, having first met him when she was Socceroos operations manager under Farina, as well as later working at senior executive level with Football Federation Australia (FFA).

When Australia was bidding for the 2018 and 2022 World Cups, Johnston volunteered to be of assistance, saying if there was anything he could do for the bid, he would be happy to help, including playing the role of ambassador.

Johnston told FFA that he knew many of the FIFA movers and shakers, and that he could walk in and get a meeting with the likes of Sepp Blatter.

Mersiades was heavily involved in the FFA bid until she was sacked in January 2010 for disagreeing with how the bid was being run.

"Ben Buckley (then FFA CEO) didn't even go to that meeting with Craig. He sent the Chief Financial Officer and me along, and the only reason the CFO came along to the meeting was because he wanted to meet Craig Johnston, not because he was relevant to the meeting. I was wheeled out because, at the time, I was truly the only football person there, I had met him previously and I could at least talk the same language."

It was here that Johnston talked up his contacts, history and credentials.

"I remember going back to Ben and saying it would be great to have Craig spruiking our bid and opening doors for us, but the attitude was – as communicated by one of our international consultants - '*We don't need f**king has-beens like that promoting our bid.*'"

"Every interaction I have had with Craig Johnston over the years, he has been nothing but supportive of Australian football. It's outrageous that he's had to apologise for that one comment, said at a time when quite frankly you could understand where he was coming from."

Johnston's clashes with Australia football officials continued, no matter if they were called the Australian Soccer Federation, Soccer Australia or Football Federation Australia.

"Yeah, there's a lot of history that people need to get cleared and I've always had this issue with the administrators, because I've always been a footballer interested in the art and craft and hard work of football.

"It gets twisted when the administrators get involved.

"Maybe that's like politicians in government. I'm a lover and a purist of the art and craft of football, the purity of the game and what it means to people. I've always respected that and always will."

George Negus speaks of Johnston's career as being the trailblazer for other Australians to follow into the United Kingdom and abroad.

"If Craig Johnston had not done what he did, and broken into the English Premiership, probably none of the Australians, none of the Bosnich's, Cahill's etcetera would have done it. He broke the soil, the kid from Newcastle could do it after years and years of trying, it just opened the door for other people."

Unfortunately for Johnston, his storied career finished without a Socceroos cap.

"Do I regret not playing for Australia? I do, but I don't regret keeping in the Middlesbrough team and keeping in the Liverpool team. I will never regret that," Johnston says.

"What was clear to me, every time I took the field with a Liverpool shirt on or a Middlesbrough shirt on, I was representing Australia, because I am a proud Australian."

Now the game has FIFA windows for international breaks, clubs having to let players go to play for their national team, as Frank Farina succinctly puts it.

"If the time was now, Craig Johnston would have played for Australia."

The final word on Johnston should come from George Negus. After nearly 40 years of friendship, a gesture at the 2006 World Cup should sum up what he means to Australian football and what Australia means to him.

"In 2006 he was in London and I was in Germany at the World Cup. I was still on the Board so I selfishly had two Socceroos shirts made, one with Negus on the back, and then I also got an official Socceroos top with Johnston on it.

"The day before the match against Italy, Craig jumped on a plane and came over to Kaiserslauten. We had a crew having lunch and a few reds and Craig joined us.

"At that lunch I made Craig stand up, close his eyes and hold his hands above his head. I slipped the official Socceroos shirt with '*Johnston*' on it over his arms and head. When he saw what he had on, he started crying, he's quite an emotional person. We all clapped and cheered. He took some time to recover.

"It was me saying to him, '*you never wore it, but you more than deserved to wear it*'."

After playing 64 games with Middlesbrough Johnston played 190 games for Liverpool between 1981-1988.

His time at the Reds included Five First Division Titles, Two League Cups, a Charity Shield, an FA Cup and a European Cup.

In a 2006 worldwide poll '*100 Players who shook the Kop*' Craig Johnston was voted the 59th best Liverpool player of all time.

Johnston has one of the best footballing résumés of any Australian.

2
England's Colonials
- Tony Dorigo

In 1991-92, the final season before the English First Division would rebrand themselves as the English Premier League, Leeds United won their third title.

Leeds would finish four points ahead of Manchester United with a star-studded team that included internationals Gordon Strachan, Gary McAllister, David Batty, Gary Speed and Eric Cantona. Player of the year for Leeds United in their title winning season of 1991-92 was an Australian - Tony Dorigo.

Born in Melbourne in 1965 to an Australian mother and an Italian immigrant father, Dorigo moved to Adelaide at a young age as his mother's family were from Peterborough in South Australia. A typical Australian sporting upbringing saw Dorigo dabble in cricket and Australian Rules football, but with an Italian father, the round ball game would become his first love.

Dorigo played for various clubs around Adelaide, teams such as Cumberland and Polonia, where his skill level was such that he always played in teams above his age group. His final move in Australian club football was to Adelaide City in the National Soccer League.

Adelaide City, formerly Juventus, is the biggest and most successful club in South Australia. It has the distinction of having more Socceroos playing for them than any other club in South Australia, and only powerhouse clubs Marconi in Sydney's west and South Melbourne have had more. The likes of Alex Tobin, Milan Ivanovic, Aurelio Vidmar, Tony Vidmar and John Aloisi have all gone through Adelaide City. Tony Dorigo and John Moriarty (later in the book) are alumni as well.

Dorigo was extremely ambitious and already starting to plot a career overseas in England.

"At 15 I was training with the first team, which was a great experience but I thought I had hit the ceiling in Australia."

Adelaide City had Englishman Justin Fashanu on loan for the 1980-81 season.

He had played for Norwich City and had just signed to Brian Clough's Nottingham Forest, becoming England's first £1 million transfer of a black footballer.

"Justin Fashanu had just come across and signed from Norwich and had scored that amazing goal, the goal of the year against Liverpool (BBC Goal of the year 1979-80). I just asked him so many things about England. I told him I just wanted to go to England too and when was the best time to do it. English football was on TV once a week and it looked amazing. That's how it all started."

The approach to English first division clubs was not unlike Craig Johnston. It all began with a letter writing campaign.

Picking the top 12 teams in the English first division Dorigo wrote three to four-page letters extolling his talents and asking for an opportunity.

Just like Johnston, only one club replied. It was Aston Villa.

"My dad and I just jumped on a plane and headed over.

"They only gave me a four-day trial. They didn't want me on a Friday because they were doing set pieces for their game the next day, so that was it."

Trialling in a Birmingham winter out of a South Australian summer would prove challenging. It was also Dorigo's first time out of Australia, but two weeks after the trial Aston Villa signed him.

"I'm not sure where they were on my list (of clubs he wrote to). They actually won the title when I went there, and then the year after they won the European Cup as well. It was amazing that it ended up being them. The setup they've got at Villa is just superb for youth. It was a great club to go to."

In 1984 Tony would make his first division debut for Aston Villa against Ipswich Town and would end up playing 111 times for the Villans in four seasons, including winning their Player of the Year in 1986.

Whilst at Aston Villa, Tony was able to travel to Italy for the first time, taking in his father's home club of Udinese on a pre-season tour. It would also set him up for a future of playing against the big players and the big teams.

"So there I am as a 17-year old kid and I'm playing against Udinese. I'm playing against this winger. He's an old guy, he has a moustache, but I'm thinking, *'I'll have him'*.

"I'm right into this guy, I'm kicking him, I'm running past him, I'm doing everything and he's swearing at me in Italian and he's going crazy at me, and I booted him again and off I go again.

"Anyway, he got taken off and afterwards they are going *'Why were you so aggressive with the great Franco Causio?'*. I thought *'Oh My God was that Franco Causio!'*. I didn't even realise."

Causio was a member of Italy's World Cup winning squad in 1982, playing 63 times for Italy as well as over 300 games for Juventus.

"Udinese tried to buy me after that game. They put an offer in, a million quid to try and buy me. That's my Dad's home town!

"I was thinking, this is kind of crazy."

It was during this time at Aston Villa that Tony got an approach from Australia to come and represent the Socceroos. Humbled and honoured, he went to his manager but was told that they wouldn't release him.

"I was asked to go and play, I think it was four to five games in a five-week period. You obviously can't go back and forth, you would have to go out there for a big chunk of time. When I look back at it we were playing, I can't remember exactly, Fiji or other teams from Oceania. At Aston Villa I'm playing Manchester United, then I'm playing Arsenal at Highbury and the manager (Tony Barton) looked at me like I was an alien when I asked him.

"He wouldn't let me go. I wanted to go, but in the end it was impossible, so I had to put that in the back of my head and just carry on. The chance was there but unfortunately it passed."

In Robert Lusetich's 1992 book *Frank Arok - My Beloved Socceroos* he claims that on a Socceroos tour of China and Europe in 1984 Arok approached Dorigo about representing Australia but was told that Dorigo wanted to represent Italy.

Dorigo didn't speak any Italian and says these claims are false.

"Italy was never part of the plan. At that age it was always Australia, I didn't think of anything else."

"I only ever wanted to play for Australia, because if you think of all the memories that I had they were of Australian football. You know Johnny Warren, John Kosmina and these types of players. And then of the course the 1974 World Cup in Germany. That what it was all about."

Not long after he knocked back the Socceroos, whilst he was doing some great things with Aston Villa in the first division, England came knocking on the door.

He was made aware that after five years of residence it was possible for him to play for any country in Great Britain. England have a history of picking naturalised players and so-called colonials in many of their sports, particularly cricket.

With the logistics of travel and club commitments ruling him out of the Socceroos, and with him in the mind of England, Dorigo went about his club career with the only thought of national selection being if he was picked for England.

Transferring to Chelsea in 1988 for £475,000, Dorigo would earn Player of the Year honours again in his first season. Although they were relegated, he helped them gain promotion the next season.

It was whilst at Chelsea, where he eventually played 146 games, that Dorigo was picked in the England squad. He earned 15 caps for England which included the 1988 European Championships in West Germany, the 1990 World Cup in Italy and the 1992 European Championships in Sweden.

Italia '90 was an amazing campaign for England, famous for the exploits of Paul Gascoigne and Gary Lineker. England lost their semi-final to eventual champions West Germany 4-3 on penalties.

After elimination at Italia '90, England were forced into the third place play-off game and Dorigo was called into the team to play against Italy. He provided the cross for David Platt to score for England in a 2-1 defeat to the hosts. Dorigo's Italian born father said it was the perfect result.

"I saw Dad and he couldn't be happier. He said everything was perfect. *'You played well and Italy won that's great!'*"

The seasons after Italia '90 were the better ones for Dorigo, transferring to Leeds from Chelsea in 1991 for £1.3 million. It was an unusual thrill for Dorigo, given his father's allegiance to the West Yorkshire club.

"Growing up in Adelaide, as a little kid, you have these dreams and things.

"When Dad talked about Leeds, I thought *'I'm not going to play for Leeds'* as they weren't in the top division. I played for Villa, I played for Chelsea, and then low and behold years later I play for Leeds and we win the title. It was nuts."

Leeds finished the 42-game season losing only four games, with 22 wins and 16 draws.

Dorigo's second season at Leeds United was the first season of the rebranded English Premier League and Leeds would end the season in 17th spot just two points clear of relegation. Nonetheless Dorigo was selected in the Premier League Team of the Year, and was selected in the England squad for the 1992 European Championships.

At the end his 1997 contract with Leeds United, Dorigo was approached to play for Torino in Italy by Scotland and Liverpool legend Graeme Souness. The two even had an unlikely South Australian connection.

Whilst Dorigo was growing up in Adelaide, Souness played six times for West Adelaide on loan in 1977 in the national football league. Italy for Dorigo though, was a tremendous thrill given his heritage.

"That was wonderful. Italian football suited me very well. I'm clearly not a big physical player nor a technical fast player. I tried to go out and just play in Italy.

"Graeme Souness had always been trying to buy me for Rangers and at various points in my career. When he went to Torino, he asked me would I like to go also. I could have gone to Middlesbrough under Bryan Robson, but they were procrastinating, so when Graeme rang up for Torino and I thought *'You know what, I know I'm 32, 33 but let's give it a go'.*

"To have another experience, it was brilliant. You learn so much by playing in another country and league. I thought I'd give it a go and I had a fantastic time, it was very different, so you're still learning.

"I really enjoyed my time. Even though I did miss the penalty in the play-off that could have got us promoted, it went really well."

The northern Italian side were in a yo-yo stage of their history. They had been relegated three times to Serie B in the ten years prior to Dorigo joining and were in a penalty shoot-out against Perugia to get promoted. Dorigo did miss that penalty but was rewarded after the season with Torino's Player of the Year award.

The following season Torino had to let Dorigo go for financial reasons, and he returned to the UK. Torino earned promotion back into the Serie A the season after Dorigo left in 1998-99.

Dorigo is filled with pride when he reflects on his European career, and rightly so. A member of a World Cup squad that made the finals, two Euro squads and Player of the Year awards at Aston Villa, Chelsea, Leeds United and Torino. His football résumé for an Australian is impressive.

"I am proud of all of that. I was player of the year when we won the title at Leeds. We had a great team then, an incredible midfield, so I did something right.

"Obviously full back is different as well, I think it's easy as an attacker or a striker to score goals and get the headlines. You just do what you do and enjoy it and I was certainly appreciated everywhere I went.

"I was very fortunate. You look back at where you start and every game of every season I knew what I was doing.

"I had dreams of scoring at Wembley of course. We didn't get to any of the big Cup finals but I did score at both ends of Wembley which was great: once in the Charity Shield and once with Chelsea against Middlesbrough in front of 80,000 people, 1-0. I mean a lot of the stuff you dream about as a kid, I ticked off.

"I will always be very grateful and thrilled to still be involved."

Dorigo would play more games at Leeds than any other of his clubs (190 in total), and on returning from Italy, he had short stints back in England with Derby County and Stoke City before retiring in 2001. It is at Leeds that he is best remembered.

Tony now works as an expert commentator across Europe and is also as an ambassador for Leeds United.

He crossed paths with Harry Kewell in his final year at Leeds and some other Socceroos who have also played for Leeds, including two Socceroos' captains, Paul Okon and Mark Viduka, as well as Jacob Burns, Hayden Foxe, Joel Griffiths, Neil Kilkenny and Patrick Kisnorbo.

It was a different time, and Australia missed out on the skills and ability of Tony Dorigo.

"When I first started out international football wasn't as clear cut as it is now. I mean, look at the nationalities in the Premier League now. Everyone flies around the world to play for their country. You go back and on you go.

"I do have some sadness in not going back and doing stuff in Australia, but the path just took me a different way," Dorigo says.

"Back then you were very much at the beck and call of the club and coordinating international calendars was very different. Now, it doesn't matter who you get called up by. There are gaps to play for your country, no problems.

"People in England say to me you must be proud to have played for England, and I was, it's a great honour and because I've lived here now so long I feel more and more English.

"But you never forget where you come from and where you were brought up."

In 2004 Leeds United produced a list of its top 100 players of all time. Tony Dorigo was voted 33rd. Australians Harry Kewell and Mark Viduka were also in the top 50. In all, he played 190 times for Leeds between 1991-1997.

3
Acceptance and Excellence – Our Indigenous stars: Perkins, Briscoe and Moriarty

Manchester United, Tottenham Hotspur, Arsenal, Everton and Preston North End. Some of the biggest clubs in the UK and Europe. Imagine if Australian players were plying their trade with these clubs now.

In the 1950s and 1960s it could have happened, when three Aboriginal boys from St Francis House in Adelaide were invited to trial with some of the biggest clubs in England.

This Anglican home near the beach housed a number of boys. Some were there with the blessing of their mothers to gain an education, others were part of the Stolen Generation. At this time they were not recognised in Australia as citizens and some had to get permission to travel with representative football sides. They could not vote and did not have the same rights as non-Indigenous Australians.

However, the players were overwhelmingly accepted into the football community. Their talent obviously helped, but with the post-World War II immigration boom, they were embraced into the fold of football clubs.

Charles Perkins, John Moriarty and Gordon Briscoe were the talented players invited to play football in the UK.

Perkins was invited to trial with Manchester United but ended up starring with top ranked amateur club Bishop Auckland.

Moriarty went to Europe but had his flight home paid for by Adelaide Juventus who wanted his services for the upcoming season. Moriarty was also picked in the squad for the Australian national team for a tour to Hong Kong, but the tour was cancelled and he was not selected again.

Briscoe played with Preston North End, but his marriage, family and education took precedence over his football.

The winter UK weather, the culture shock and what was happening with Australian politics meant that these great Indigenous Australians all had other priorities.

The political, academic and business achievements of Perkins, Briscoe and Moriarty far outdid anything they could have even imagined getting from football.

As it stands Moriarty was the first Aboriginal Australian selected for the Socceroos, but the honour of the first Aboriginal to play for Australia went to Harry Williams in 1970. Williams was part of our 1974 World Cup squad. He was later joined by the likes of Frank Farina who debuted in 1984, Kasey Wehrman in 1998, Jade North in 2002, Travis Dodd in 2006, David Williams in 2008 and Adam Sarota in 2011.

How did it come about that these boys would play the world game?

Adjoining St Francis House in Semaphore was an open paddock. Port Thistle Soccer Club were using it as a training ground. By chance a South Australian Under 18 representative side was training on the ground and they asked the boys, who were watching them train, for a scratch match to help them sharpen their skills. The St Francis boys had never played football before, but they went on to dominate the pickup game, piling on more than seven goals to zero against a representative team no less!

Port Thistle then invited some of the older boys to play in their senior side and when Port Thistle was promoted to the South Australian first division they were faced with a dilemma. Every first division side required juniors and Port Thistle didn't have any, so they started recruiting the talented kids from St Francis House.

"The property (St Francis House) had an amount of land which was part of the stevedoring property of Port Adelaide," Gordon Briscoe recalls.

"In that time, the early 50s, draft horses were used on the wharves everywhere, both for timber and for wool and those sorts of things. It wasn't unusual to see 10-15 draft horses bringing things from factories around Adelaide to Port Adelaide.

"In the evening the draft horses were put off in these paddocks. There was a team called Port Thistle which was a breakaway from Port Adelaide Soccer Club. They went top of the second division and were looking to become part of the first division, but they had to have junior teams and they had to have a field of their own.

"They approached the church as they knew there were a lot of kids there, and they could rent part of the property that was set aside for the horses. So I started off in the junior ranks of Port Thistle and played soccer on Saturdays."

Perkins, Briscoe and Moriarty would all develop football skills but at the same time, develop life skills and aspirations for higher education, enabling them to become leaders within the Aboriginal community, all thanks to football.

According to John Maynard, author of *The Aboriginal Soccer Tribe*, each of these players had different abilities on the pitch.

"Charlie was the real standout, Johnny had wonderful skills on the ball but if you were going to pick a team, any team, Charles Perkins would have been the first player you would pick. He was the standout, so strong. He got picked for NSW when he came over," John recalled from his book research.

"Gordon wasn't at the same level from observations that I've read and the interviews that I've done. But Gordon was a bloody good player. I mean to play at that level and in England with Preston North End. They were in first division then, it just shows the quality of player he was. But as far as Charlie and John go, they would have been well worth an Australian shirt."

Perkins was the first to head overseas with his football. In 1957, a visiting scout from Everton saw him play in Adelaide and offered to pay half his fare to England for a trial. Perkins was 21, travelled via boat from Melbourne to Genoa, then a train to Paris and then on to London. Perkins travelled on the cheapest fare, suffered severe seasickness and then had his belongings stolen in Paris. He arrived in London with just the clothes he was wearing.

Perkins battled it out at Everton without much luck. The weather, homesickness and a lack of fitness didn't help his cause.

From Everton, Perkins joined leading amateur club Bishop Auckland and played a few seasons there with distinction. Bishop Auckland is in County Durham in the north east of England. Perkins' time at Bishop Auckland saw Manchester United send him a letter requesting that he trial with the Red Devils, but his experience in playing football at Oxford University lit the flame for some new ambitions. Perkins wanted a university education.

In the 1950s and 1960s Zlatko Drapac was Branko Filipi's right hand man on the committee at Adelaide Croatia Soccer Club. Working as club secretary, Drapac's football knowledge was supported by Filipi's wealth. Drapac remembers how they got Perkins to the club, straight from Bishop Auckland.

"Charlie was in England and didn't have money to come back to Australia. He was homesick. His mate Gordon Briscoe came to me and said *'Zak, I have a very good player in England. He's playing with Bishop Auckland and he wants to come back to Australia but he can't, he's buggered. He's a very good bloke and a very good player, he'll be a top player in your team.'*

"Then I talked to Filipi and he said straight away to bring him back before someone else gets him. And we did. Straight away, we sent for him and he came here. There was a big reception when he came here and I named him playing coach and captain of the team."

Perkins loved it around the football community. The level of acceptance was something he didn't experience in everyday Australian life. According to Drapac, the Croatians accepted who he was.

"There was a low appreciation of anything Aboriginal people tried to do. We didn't agree with that. That fit very well into our community and were appreciated for who they are and what they can do."

It was at this time with Adelaide Croatia that Perkins met his wife Eileen.

"I'd never seen a game of soccer, I was into Aussie Rules being South Australian.

"He had certain skills and a streak that was able to bring out the best in players."

Once Perkins and Eileen were married, his desire for higher education continued.

"He wanted to go to university and was inspired by playing against a university team at Oxford."

The Charlie Perkins Scholarship now supports a postgraduate scholarship for Aboriginal and Torres Strait Islander people wanting to attend Oxford, but for Perkins to get the degree he wanted, he had to move to Sydney.

Drapac arranged the transfer.

"I sold him for £250 to Pan-Hellenic in Sydney, and he went and got his degree."

Perkins joined the Pan-Hellenic Club in Sydney. Such was his talents on the field he was captain within three months and captain coach within six. According to Eileen he was really embraced by the club.

"The Greeks in Sydney thought it was marvellous to have a university man in their team. A lot of them were labourers who were working to put their kids through university. They understood it was pretty amazing.

"There wasn't much else in our lives, he was studying and we were very poor. It (football) became our life really."

In 1966, Perkins became the first Aboriginal person to get a university degree in Australia.

He went on to continue playing football throughout his life but he is best known for being a civil rights activist who dedicated his life to achieving justice for Aboriginal and Torres Strait Islander people. He was later head of the federal Department of Aboriginal Affairs and Chairman of the Aboriginal Development Commission and Aboriginal Hostels.

Perkins was Chairman of Canberra City soccer club in the National Soccer League and a vice-President of the Australian Soccer Federation.

If it wasn't for his work ambitions, he had the potential to be considered for the national team. A tough player who never took a backwards step, he represented both South Australia and New South Wales.

According to Adelaide Croatia's secretary Drapac he was a brilliant player.

"I think he was close to being selected in the Australian team. He definitely was one of the top players of his time."

* * *

Gordon Briscoe played with Perkins at Adelaide Croatia, a solid and reliable player described as one that was always picked to play in the first team. Soon after Perkins returned to Australia, Briscoe got itchy feet to travel overseas.

"People whispered in my ear, indicating that soccer in England was an opportunity and I would do better there than I would in Australia. I had a little bit of money saved up. One of my friends at that time was an Englishman who had a family in Hemel Hempstead (about forty minutes north west of London), so that is where I started off."

Arriving in the UK summer of 1960, Briscoe started his sporting adventure abroad by first playing cricket in the UK as a fast bowler. In Briscoe's first winter he played football for an amateur team called Hemel Hempstead Rovers.

"I scored a few goals and someone asked me to have a trial match for Preston North End."

Preston North End famously had Australian Joe Marston play there for five seasons in the 1950s, so trialling another Aussie made sense to them.

"In late 1960-61 I was in the third side (at Preston). A lot of people thought I was much better than most Australians that came over.

"I was not really robust as I thought I was, my ankles were not good. I had opportunities to go up in Preston but unfortunately I never reached the heights I thought that I would like to be."

Playing on the freezing grounds of the United Kingdom didn't help and playing with younger teammates was also a struggle.

"I was being selected for the junior sides. The Midlands are a very cold place with frozen fields, which didn't suit me at all with my skinny legs!

"I never had any feelings for international or first division sides. After I got there my injuries were cooling down my enthusiasm and I had to work as well. My ambitions changed."

By ambitions Briscoe meant family life. He had met his English wife Norma and had a son as well. Working and caring for them became the priority.

"I went out, I got married, I had a child to look after then. I had calls from Charlie to come back to Canterbury Bankstown (in Sydney). So we came back to Australia in 1964 and I went to Canterbury-Bankstown.

"However, I was unable to get payment so I had to get a job. That was the end of my career in senior football!"

Briscoe's academic and professional achievements far outweigh what he could have achieved on the pitch, becoming the first Aboriginal to gain a PhD (in History), which he achieved at the Australian National University in Canberra.

* * *

'*Congratulations John, they have selected you for Australia!*'
With those words from South Australian football chairman Bob Telfer, John Moriarty

was the first Aboriginal selected for the Socceroos.

Moriarty was picked in the Australia squad that was to tour South East Asia in 1960 playing against the likes of Hong Kong.

After the squad was announced, FIFA banned Australia from international competition because its club sides did not pay transfer fees for footballers from Europe who were making their way to Australia.

These European players were forging new lives in Australia whilst also playing club football, and included the likes of Austrian Leo Baumgartner, who would lift the standard and the crowds in the local game within Australia.

This non-payment of fees robbed Moriarty and others of their Socceroos claims at the peak of their playing ability. It was an opportunity lost.

When Moriarty was removed from his mother, aged only four, he was first sent to Mulgoa in New South Wales, before becoming part of St Francis House in Semaphore around 11 years of age.

His football progressed through Adelaide with the likes of Port Thistle and Port Adelaide, which saw Moriarty eventually picked to play for South Australia in Perth against Western Australia.

At this stage in Australia's history, Aboriginal people needed permission to travel interstate.

After representing South Australia, Moriarty was approached to play for Adelaide Juventus (now Adelaide City) and he joined the Italian backed club.

"Adelaide Juventus was very good. I was admired there, I was respected. Similarly I respected the club and their supporters."

It was as a Juventus player that John was picked in the Australian squad.

"Bob Telfer who was the chairman of South Australian soccer. He came up to me after the final game, the game that I played in and he said *'Congratulations John, they have selected you for Australia!'* and I said *'Thank you Mr Telfer, thanks for that'.*"

With the bond from St Francis House very strong, the first thing Moriarty asked Telfer was whether Perkins was also selected. Moriarty thought he was good enough.

"Charlie wasn't picked for Australia, just one of those things. Selection systems are strange."

After the national trials in 1960, Moriarty was given the opportunity to go to the United Kingdom and trial for some powerhouse clubs such as Arsenal, Tottenham and Everton.

"When I was recommended to train with those clubs, they accepted me because a journalist (UK based Bernard Moss) had seen me play, but I was completing my apprenticeship as I had no skills, nothing to sell other than football.

"So I stuck to a fitting and turning course and became a qualified tradesman. It wasn't really my focus from then on, because I saw so much through football and realised I could learn more through football.

"I travelled over there to hopefully trial for them (in the UK), but then I got a message from Australia saying we (Adelaide Juventus) are playing in the Australian championships and we would like to fly you back and have you play.

"After being over there, I thought '*I haven't got a degree*' and I wanted a university degree, but I still wanted to play football. I ended up making the decision to come back."

Not unlike Perkins, Moriarty was flown home to play club football in Adelaide where his personal ambitions revolved around education and acceptance.

"Charlie was the first one to get a degree. I was the first one in Adelaide, and Gordon got one later on.

"Charlie was a real powerhouse, politically, and we got on very well."

Moriarty is still involved with football through the John Moriarty Foundation, believing that if opportunities are afforded to Aboriginal kids through football, then the sky is the limit.

"We want to give Aboriginal kids opportunities. The game gave me opportunities but we had to fight for them. Hopefully the program we have will get them playing, representing their communities, Aboriginal people and Australians."

***

The post playing careers of Charlie Perkins, Gordon Briscoe and John Moriarty are best summed up by Professor John Maynard of the University of Newcastle in Australia, who says all three credit football as their big break.

"The three of them were major players in Aboriginal affairs and all of them acknowledge that it was football that gave them that stage and that opportunity to step into that space.

"The racism and the prejudice and the oppression; the way they were looked at and the way they were treated on the streets; the migrant communities just completely opened up to them and offered them unparalleled opportunities and acceptance.

"They had never experienced that before. John Moriarty was suddenly eating at Italian restaurants and taken to Italian tailors and being fitted out in suits. Charlie Perkins and Gordon Briscoe experienced the same thing with the Croatians, and Charlie also with the Greeks.

"That experience gave them a much wider understanding of the world and appreciation of things around them, instead of inside the racist bubble that they thought for a long time that they were trapped in.

"All three went on to university education; Charlie and Johnny and Gordon when they first started coming through, they had to do it tougher, but they worked really hard at it.

"I certainly know from Gordon's experiences, he really, really put so much time in his education and gaining that experience. Gordon was instrumental in the Aboriginal Legal Service and the Aboriginal Medical Service.

"All those things that were set up and started in Redfern in the late 60s and early 70s, all were repercussions of these guys experiences, first as footballers, and then their experience through education."

* * *

Other key figures from St Francis House included Harold Thomas, who designed the iconic Aboriginal flag, Max Wilson who played Under 17s football for South Australia and Gerry Hill who became a junior football coach, having a heavy influence over the developing career of South Australian star and future Socceroo captain John Kosmina.

4
Green and Gold Goalkeeping Glut – Didulica and Ilic

Australia has always been blessed with an abundance of great goalkeepers, from cricketer Ken Grieves lining up in England for Bolton Wanderers and Wigan Athletic in the 1940s and 1950s, to domestic champions Ron Lord, Jack Reilly and Jim Fraser.

It was around the 1990s that it really started to become a production line for Australia.

Since Mark Bosnich's debut with the national team in 1990 to Matty Ryan defending the Asian Cup in 2019, the Socceroos used 19 goalkeepers in A-internationals. A dozen more goalkeepers plied their trade in Europe and never received a cap in an A-international for the Socceroos.

Since Bosnich's debut, Clint Bolton and Dean Anastasiadis are the only Socceroos who never played overseas, but both were domestic champions of the highest quality.

The 'keepers that missed out on Socceroos caps were on the books of famous European clubs, such as Celtic, Leeds United, West Ham, Everton, Charlton Athletic, Ajax Amsterdam and Juventus.

Two of these Australian goalkeepers ended up representing other countries, Croatia and the Federal Republic of Yugoslavia (later changed to Serbia and Montenegro and now Serbia), but for different reasons.

Joey Didulica was born and raised in Geelong, the younger brother of Australian football administrator John Didulica. He would learn his craft with North Geelong Croatia, before heading to the National Soccer League with Melbourne Knights. After 60 games with the Knights, Didulica earned a dream move abroad signing with Ajax Amsterdam in Holland in 1999.

Didulica was part of the Olyroos squad leading up to the Sydney Olympics in 2000, but a stress fracture of his tibia ruled him out of the tournament. Didulica then went back to Europe, worked hard on his rehab and then harder on his game. His dedication earning him selection in the Ajax first team, playing in the Champions League in the process.

It was about this time that Croatia came calling. Playing at Ajax with Didulica at the time was a Swedish player of Bosnian and Croatian descent, Zlatan Ibrahimovic.

"The Croatian team came circling. They came out to Amsterdam to talk to me and find out where my family was from. At the same time Zlatan Ibrahimovic was there, so we both sat down with the Croatian national team, the two of us. They wanted to know if we would play for Croatia.

"I had a lot of meetings with the Croatian national team whilst I was at Ajax. At that stage I wasn't called up to play for them, but they were heading into the European championships of 2004."

It was around this time that Socceroos head coach Frank Farina had a star-studded team of overseas based Australians to choose from. However, a lack of funds, fragile administration at the Board level and a reluctance for clubs to release players made his job extremely tough.

"I spoke to Frank and I did get selected for the Australian team when they played against England in 2003. They even produced a shirt for me but I didn't go to the game.

"I wasn't sure (about Australia) as I was still interested in the Croatian national team and to see where that was headed.

"Then in 2004 the Croatian delegates said "*Joey, we promise you are going to go to the European Championships with Croatia in Portugal,*" and that was too good to refuse. I decided I wanted to be a Croatian national."

Part of Didulica's decision was the state of the game in Australia.

"In 2004 there wasn't even a league in Australia. Mark Bosnich was an Australian international for seven years and he played 17 games.

"The big players were not even coming to play for the national team. They hadn't qualified for a World Cup for 30 years. Soccer in Australia was a shambles.

"In 2004 there were only two or three international games. I mean Archie Thompson was playing and scoring 13 goals in a game. It was a joke. Even the national team players at that stage would have said the same thing."

Another reason Didulica chooe to play for Croatia was their approach and how they seduced their players. Being in Europe they were able to do this quite easily.

"The Croatian national team were very persuasive. They took you out to dinner, they called you up every game and were really on top of it. Almost like courting you know. That was what you want as a player. Everybody wants to feel like they're special and needed. They played that well."

Croatia's World Cup and Euro squads nearly always feature players of Croatian heritage who were not born in the country, but their courting didn't work on Ibrahimovic. Didulica thinks that he was a different case.

"I didn't think he felt as Croatian as I did. He was divided. His father was Bosnian, his mum was Croatian and he lived in Sweden. Playing for Sweden wasn't as bad as playing for Australia at that time. They were qualifying for tournaments."

Didulica's upbringing in club football in Australia was nearly always about representing Croatia too, with many Australian football clubs founded along ethnic lines.

"With my choice about playing for Croatia, I spoke to many players who were faced with the same predicament. Joe Simunic was the same, as was Ante Seric. We grew up part of the Croatian community, we all played for Croatian clubs. When you were playing for Croatian clubs back in the day, you were playing against Brunswick Juventus, Preston Makedonia and you were playing against all these ethnic clubs.

"We were representing Croatia when we played. Geelong Croatia, Melbourne Croatia. Every game was like you were playing in a European Qualifier or a European game.

"My heart was always with playing for Croatia growing up, and the pinnacle of that was playing for the Croatian national team. I was born in Australia and living in Australia, I mean I love Australia, I live here, there is no better country in the world.

"But when it came to football, my heart was Croatia through and through."

This sense of nationalism was the cause of some gentle ribbing from his teammates, with Joey wearing a necklace of the Croatian flag.

"We were different, I was Australian Croatian. We had German Croatians who came with a whole different mentality. I was very passionate about Croatia, loved the country, loved the people. I loved everything about it.

"But they just looked at me and go '*Mate, you're from the past*' wearing a necklace of the Croatian emblem; they go '*What are you wearing that for?*' like an Australian wearing an Australian flag around their neck – who does that?!"

The argument that Didulica chose Croatia over Australia due to him falling behind Schwarzer and Kalac in the pecking order riles Didulica.

"One can say '*Yeah we had Bosnich, Schwarzer and Kalac*', but if you look back, in 2003 I was the only one playing Champions League football.

"I was young and I was at Ajax Amsterdam. I was definitely in contention."

When Didulica looks back on his career that saw him play club football in Australia, Holland, Belgium and Austria, he can add a trip to the 2004 European Championships and the 2006 World Cup as part of the Croatian squad as career highlights. He earned four caps for Croatia in the process.

Didulica was one of three Australian-born players in the Croatian squad at the 2006 World Cup in Germany, along with Ante Seric and Joe Simunic.

Unlike Seric and Simunic, Didulica never made any Victorian or Australian representative squads or development programs growing up. He learned his craft in club football before heading to Europe. He was also on the bench for that famous 2-2 draw when Australia played Croatia to make it through to the Round of 16, Australia having many squad members of Croatian descent.

"A very surreal day.

"It was like being at Somers Street at Knights Stadium – watching Mark Viduka and Joe Simunic in a practice game."

* * *

Sasa Ilic would divide his childhood years between his place of birth Melbourne and his parents' home town of Belgrade.

Ilic says they moved back to Belgrade on three occasions when he was eight, 14 and 17. As a junior he made Victorian representative sides, including a team that would face a New South Wales team that featured Mark Bosnich. With the constant to-ing and fro-ing between countries, he fell off the representative radar. As a young adult about to enter university, Ilic moved back to Europe, football being secondary to his education and his socialising.

From the most humble of beginnings, to chance encounters, dogged determination and a will to succeed, Ilic would find himself on the main stage of Wembley and eventually becoming a Premier League goalkeeper. His football career reads almost like a movie script. It is probably worth a book on its own.

After the fall of Yugoslavia in the early 1990s, Ilic went to visit his sisters in London, asked a bar manager if he knew of any clubs that needed a goalkeeper, and within two years he was trialling at Aston Villa as an understudy to Mark Bosnich. He ended up a football hero, saving the final penalty at Wembley that saw his team Charlton Athletic get promoted to the Premier League.

Ilic was in Yugoslavia playing for Partizan Belgrade before a move to FK Radnički saw him break into the first team at 19 years of age. Things were going great for Ilic but within 12 months of being there the country started disintegrating.

"War. It was pretty sad when it comes to ethnic conflict. The aftermath and effects of the sanctions and embargos had a profound effect on the place. Refugees coming from Croatia and Bosnia into Serbia. You had a whole country just change, literally overnight.

"Coming from Australia it was challenging. All of a sudden there's electricity surges and product rations. Things like this. Detergent was deemed to be a luxury item."

With the uncertainty going on in Yugoslavia, Ilic decided a visit to his sisters in London was in order. He spent a great deal of time partying whilst staying on their couch. It was just before he was due to leave the UK that he ventured into a pub, asked if anyone needed a goalkeeper, and the seeds were sown for his UK career when he started talking to the bar manager.

"We were at this bar called *'Football Football'*. We just started chatting and one thing led to another and I mentioned to him that I was playing top league football in Yugoslavia and I would love to come and play here.

"His name was Mike Trussent. He was manager of this pub and he was also appointed manager of this non-league football club in East Sussex in a town called Hastings. He said *"You know we're looking for a goalkeeper. We've got these two owners who won the lottery; one is a huge business man in that part of the world. If you pass me a video tape of you playing and I can pass that on to them."*

The team was St Leonards Football Club, owned by Leon Sheperdson who ran a timber company in Hastings. As soon as Ilic got back to Belgrade he put together a video compilation package of his saves from his time in Yugoslavia and sent it to Sheperdson.

Sheperdson liked what he saw and invited Ilic to join St Leonards immediately. He was hesitant as he wanted to finish his university degree and had a year to go on his football contract with FK Radnički. Sheperdson made some arrangements which convinced him to head west.

"There was no prosperity there anymore (in Belgrade). So I borrowed money from a loan shark to buy out my own contract. It was 5,000 deutschmarks, which was literally a couple of thousand pounds to buy out my contract.

"I packed my bag and St Leonards paid for my flight. They had someone meet me at the airport and drove me down. So I met this guy who said *'I saw this video, I saw this sparkle in your eye, this hunger in you and this is what we want in my team.'*

"They also paid for my final year of tuition at university."

Playing non-league football in England was somewhat of a cultural shock for Ilic, but he saw it as a great way to learn the English game. His obvious talent and ability shone through. In that one season he was voted the best non-league goal keeper in the southern part of England.

This helped him attract attention from some of the higher clubs in England, including Aston Villa.

"Aston Villa scouts were following me and they sent the goalkeeping coach Paul Barron over to watch this one game. It was the last game of the season and he approached me afterwards asking if I would like to come on trial with Aston Villa, I'm like *'Yeah of course I would.'*"

Ilic joined Aston Villa for their pre-season as he trialled with the Villans. He was training everyday with Mark Bosnich, a fellow Aussie who he had played against as a kid.

"Two very different paths, but we had met at one destination."

There was talk that Bosnich would be leaving Aston Villa. He was at the peak of his powers and attracting interest from a number of top clubs, so Ilic was brought in to trial, just in case he left.

It was an amazing step up from his time in Hastings.

"Two months before I was playing non-league football and now I am going out for dinners with guys like Dwight Yorke. It was a dream come true for me."

Bosnich would stay at Villa for one more season, before his famed move to Manchester United.

For Ilic and Aston Villa things didn't work out so well. He played in one friendly but wasn't considered for their squad. The managers tried to help him find a new club with options like Plymouth and then Oxford.

"One of the managers said you could go to Oxford. That was like going from Premier League to Third Division and I didn't really like Oxford, from their training facilities, mentality and everything else.

"It was like jumping from a thoroughbred horse onto a donkey."

Self-belief was never an issue for Ilic. He felt he belonged at the top level and managed to contact a director at Charlton Athletic, then in England's Second Division known as the Championship, asking if he could trial with them.

"I had just come off two months of pre-season training at Aston Villa I was fit as a fiddle and raring to go. This was within a month of the start of the season so they put me in the reserve team with the kids and that kind of stuff, they couldn't score a goal past me and they were asking '*Who is this guy?*'.

"After training the guy said, *'You've done well come back to training again tomorrow'*. I came back and they still couldn't score a goal past me. On the third day they started to ask me, '*Where have you come from?*' They were getting curious as I was obviously a talent."

Charlton kept asking Ilic to come back and train, but he had no contract and was paying his own way to get there. His determination and form saw him boldly just ask them to offer him a contract. With none forthcoming, Ilic asked if he could continue training with them until he could find another club. It was his form on the training track that kept him there and would eventually lead to him signing a week-to-week contract.

"I would go to training and had nothing to lose. I really got on well with the managers and the players; the rapport happened naturally. Then when we would pick sides at the end of training I would get picked in the first two goalkeepers, that was the impact I had."

But it was getting harder and harder for Ilic to get by. He was still sleeping on his sisters' couch in Putney and was even applying for jobs at one of the leisure centres in Putney just to have some spare cash. But as fate would have it, the form of Charlton's top two goalkeepers started to wane. Ilic got a look in.

First the goalkeeper, fellow Australian Andy Petterson got dropped. Then the reserve 'keeper Mike Somerton wasn't performing either and was injured. All of a sudden Ilic became part of the set up in the reserve team.

"I made it into the reserve team and for seven or eight games I didn't concede a goal. I was playing out of my skin. I was having a really good season."

So well was Ilic playing that he was promoted to reserve goalkeeper, on the bench for Charlton's first team.

"I found myself going to away games and being on the bench in front of 30,000 people. It was my dream come true."

The first team debut for Ilic for Charlton came in an away game against Stoke. He found out about his start in the pre-game meeting at the hotel when the first team manager, Alan Curbishley, announced it.

"I played that game and I was man of the match. In my first game."

In the English Championship, the top two teams are automatically promoted to the Premier League, with teams placed third through to sixth involved in play-offs to decide the third promoted team, with the last spot being decided via a final play-off match at Wembley Stadium.

Leading up to the play-offs, Charlton had an amazing run of form and they ended the regular season in fourth position. This set up home and away semi-finals to be played against Ipswich Town.

They won the first leg away 1-0 and then the second at home 1-0. Ilic set a record of ten consecutive clean sheets in the process!

"Leading up to Wembley, I played 18 games and in 14 of those I kept clean sheets"

Sunderland would be their opponent in the final. The Black Cats had finished the season in third place, accounting for Sheffield United in their semi-finals.

The Championship decider at Wembley is often referred to as the most expensive game in football. The dividends and revenue clubs receive in the Premier League from media rights is worth tens of millions of pounds. The stakes are incredibly high.

The final was an absolute goal-fest in front of 77,739 people at Wembley. Ilic let in four goals, coming after ten games without conceding a goal.

In a see-sawing affair, Charlton scored the first goal to take the lead but were chasing Sunderland the rest of the game at 1-2 and 2-3. After 90 minutes with the scores tied at 3-3 the game went into extra time.

Charlton again trailed 3-4 in extra time, before Clive Mendonca nailed his third goal to equalise for Charlton yet again.

The match finished 4-4 after extra time and would head to penalties.

"It was one of those games that will live in the hearts of Charlton for many, many years. We were playing at Wembley and goals were flying in at both ends. It was the first goal I had conceded in ten games after 900 and something minutes of clean sheets.

"Once I conceded, they kept coming in. "

Promotion was now down to penalties, Charlton taking the first and scoring. Sunderland did the same.

Both teams scored with their first six spot kicks. Both 'keepers were outsmarted, with only Ilic managing to get a hand on one of them.

"Every single penalty was superbly struck. From our end and from their end,"

After Charlton kicked the next penalty to go ahead 7-6, Ilic found a bizarre method in trying to thwart Sunderland's next kick.

"I saw this little penny shining at the back of the net and I picked it up and I flicked it. I went heads left, tails right.

"The penalty was struck to my left and I had made my mind up. As soon as he struck it my body position was going that way anyway.

"It was one of the worst penalty kicks in the history of Wembley. I happened to be there. If I went the other way, nobody would have thought twice about it but I obviously chose the right way.

"I caught the ball and ever since then I've been feted for that penalty save."

Football people will tell you that penalties are a lottery or even a coin toss. Ilic proved that on the big stage.

"People tend to recognise me for that penalty save. Even today after 20 years, people are still remembering that game. It's good to be part of history in something that will live in the memories of both teams for a very long time."

Ilic prefers to look fondly back at his time with Charlton and that save, more so than his two caps for FR Yugoslavia

"My first cap was a friendly game against Israel; it was a non-event really.

"My first cap for the qualifiers for 2002 was against Russia. It was honestly like two club teams coming together in front of 20-30,000 people. It was a complete contrast to the games I was used to playing in the UK. The pitch wasn't even watered down, the ball would stick to the grass. It was just a non-event, there were so many problems with the federation at the time.

"It was the football association of Serbia at the time, they had this manager who nobody liked. He upset a lot of people. We had a bad result, they got rid of him and put someone else in afterwards. Then each manager had their agents who needed to have their players playing in order to sell them.

"That's how it works. After that one game, that's it, I was never to be seen in the national team again.

"The only reason they called me up the first time around was because I was the only goalkeeper from that part of the world playing in the best league in the world and I had a lot of media attention. They didn't put me on the bench, they put me in to start. It was to keep the reporters and others quiet.

"But I was a rogue who came into the system and nobody wanted me there."

Ilic was never spoken to or in their thinking of the Socceroos, and he puts it down to the quality of Australian goalkeeping talent at the time.

"They had Mark Schwarzer, Mark Bosnich and John Filan - he was an amazing goalkeeper, what a goalkeeper John was! There were a lot of goalkeepers in that era, late '90s early 2000s who were top players, regarded as top-notch players. There were definitely a lot of talented Australian players at that time."

Reflecting on his career, Ilic is proud of his achievements and has no regrets.

"If I was in with the right crowd at the time maybe I could have had a more prosperous career. Too proud, too young, did it on my own, did it my way, and I wouldn't change anything. How I made it, how I succeeded, it was meant to be like that."

5
Goals gone missing – Porta, Smeltz, Vieri

15 November 2005 is a famous date in Australian football history. Australia took on Uruguay in Sydney, the second leg of the final World Cup qualifier to go to Germany in 2006. Uruguay had won the World Cup twice; this tiny South American country of 4,000,000 people always punch above their weight in world football. They see it as their right to always qualify for World Cup finals and their fans are as passionate as any in the world.

On Uruguayan television that night, a leading striker from the Uruguayan domestic league was wearing a green and gold shirt and barracking for the Socceroos. His name was Richard Porta.

Porta was born in Sydney to Uruguayan parents and moved to Uruguay at a young age. He played his youth football with Club Atletico River Plate and would go on to represent them with some distinction, scoring 41 goals in 78 appearances between 2001 and 2007. Porta's nickname in Uruguay was '*El Canguru*' which is Spanish for '*The Kangaroo*'.

Porta had flirtations with the national teams of both Uruguay and Australia without earning a senior cap with either.

When the Australian Under 17 team was in Montevideo in 1999, Porta was allegedly called in to train with the Joeys, as they are known. In 2003 he played three games with the Uruguayan Under 20 team.

Following Australia's failed campaign at the 2007 Asian Cup, captain Mark Viduka retired and did not appear for the Socceroos again. During the tenure of coaches Pim Verbeek and Holger Osieck, Australia were always looking for another avenue to goal.

Journalist, the late Mike Cockerill, was on a campaign to get Richard Porta into the Socceroos squad. Boosted by his part in getting Tim Cahill into the national team (see the later chapter '*Righting the Wrongs*') Cockerill stepped up again, constantly asking the Socceroos coaching staff about Porta and if he was being considered for selection given his goal scoring form.

Verbeek famously retorted to Cockerill in a press conference *"We are not selecting players based on YouTube clips".*

Meanwhile, Porta had been called into a couple of Uruguayan squads for home based friendlies. He was an unused substitute in a game against South Africa in 2007.

In 2011 Porta could see his opportunity for international football slowly slipping away with Uruguay. With Pim Verbeek no longer coaching Australia, he was starting to think about making himself available for selection with Holger Osieck's Socceroos.

Osieck stated that they had started to monitor his form and progress in Uruguay and Porta then made a big money move to play football in the Middle East.

According to journalist Dominic Bossi, this is when the Socceroos could have really used his services up front.

"There was a period around the end of Verbeek's tenure and the start of Holger's tenure when Richard Porta was just scoring for fun (in Dubai).

"We really didn't have anyone for that centre forward role. Harry Kewell was played there, out of position. Bruce Djite was tried. Nikita Rukavytsya was tried there, and Scott McDonald was used very poorly by Pim Verbeek.

"Josh Kennedy had some injury problems around the same time. Alex Brosque was getting a run around at that time as centre forward, Archie Thompson was used a fair bit as well. There wasn't a consistent number 9, there was always a stop gap or a short-term solution."

With Porta looking to throw his lot in with Australia, an informal meeting was arranged with a member of the Socceroos coaching staff in the United Arab Emirates.

Porta arrived early at the café and was kept waiting. No one from Australian football turned up.

Porta was hugely disappointed. He retired from playing altogether in 2017 never having played for Australia or Uruguay.

***

Shane Smeltz grew up in Queensland, but he is not a typical Queenslander.

He was born in the former West Germany to an American father stationed there in the Army and an English mother. Smeltz arrived in Auckland, New Zealand on his mother's New Zealand passport as a 12 month old, living there until aged six, when his family then moved to Queensland.

"I played my first couple of years of football in New Zealand, then we moved to Australia.

"We travelled around a bit in Queensland, settled in Cairns for a little while, then we moved down to Brisbane. By the age of 10 I was in Brisbane, then we settled on the Gold Coast. It was pretty much home from then on. A bit of travel for a kid, but I always played football and tried to find myself a home through football."

A talented junior footballer, Smeltz dreamt of one day playing for Australia.

"I was just a kid growing up in Australia and wanted to play for Australia. That was all I saw. I lived and played here. All my friends were Australian. To be honest, I felt as Australian as anyone. I had been here since I was six.

"I remember buying one of the Aussie kits, the old painted one (known as the 'spew kit'). I loved that shirt, I was running around the backyard with that with no thoughts of playing for New Zealand."

Firmly established with a home on the Gold Coast and playing football locally, Smeltz was went to the same school as world champion surfer Mick Fanning.

"You never knew what he would become, but he was only at school part-time because he was surfing so much. He loved football as well.

Smeltz started to attract attention with his football talents, making the representative side for the Gold Coast region and from there the Queensland Under 15s.

As his football developed, he was invited to join the Queensland Academy of Sport. He would drive up to Brisbane with future Socceroo Shane Stefanutto from the Gold Coast to train three times a week.

At the time the Queensland Academy of Sport team, or QAS, would play the curtain raiser games to the Brisbane Strikers in the National Soccer League. Some of the QAS alumni of that time included Jade North, Jon McKain, Matt McKay and Wayne Shroj. From here Smeltz and the QAS team would travel around the country, playing the likes of the Australian Institute of Sport and other National Soccer League youth teams.

Smeltz's form developed enough to warrant an invitation to trial at the Australian Institute of Sport in Canberra, a fertile breeding ground for Australian football talent in the 1990s, along with teammate, Daryl Hathaway.

Hathaway made it, Smeltz did not.

Smeltz returned to Brisbane an the QAS/Brisbane Strikers arrangement and started playing senior football in the state league at age 18. From here he was picked up by Brisbane Strikers coach, John Kosmina.

Around the same time, the Australian Under 20 selectors were starting to put together a squad and Smeltz was hoping to be in the mix.

"There was a time when the young national team set-up would contact the NSL coaches and clubs, asking who they wanted to bring in. There were five boys that got drafted in (from the Strikers), but I wasn't one of them."

Thinking that there may be an issue between himself and Kossie, Smeltz was annoyed that some of his teammates made the cut and he missed out.

However, not contemplating anything other than working hard to realise his dream of making it as a professional footballer, Smeltz's luck was about to change.

He received a phone call out of the blue from New Zealand head coach Ken Dugdale. Smeltz was asked if he would like to join the All Whites Under 20 camp.

How did it come about?

An enterprising relative in New Zealand made the New Zealand Federation aware of Smeltz's eligibility for the All Whites, and passed on Smeltz's details.

"I had never played for any national team squad and then you get a call from the head coach. I was quite impressed. He said *"Would you like to come into an Under 20s camp going away to New Caledonia, playing for the region to go through to qualify for the Under 20s World Cup?".*"

Finally feeling some love, Smeltz had a decision to make.

Would he try and earn some recognition in the country he grew up in and aspired to play for, or play representative football right now, with New Zealand? Ken Dugdale also floated the possibility of senior selection, saying if he did well in the underage sides he would be seriously considered for the senior team.

"I saw a bit of a pathway there which I didn't have previously. It was an easy decision for me at the time."

Australia's move into the Asian Football Confederation certainly helped New Zealand along the way once Smeltz made the senior side.

Before Australia's move to the Asian confederation it was always Australia and New Zealand fighting over who would win the Oceania confederation, with Australia coming out on top more often than not. The Oceania winner would earn a place at the Confederations Cup and a half spot or play-off to make the World Cup.

In 2009, with Australia qualifying through Asia for the first time, New Zealand played a home and away tie against Bahrain to qualify for the 2010 World Cup in South Africa. After a 0-0 draw in Manama, over 35,000 fans packed the 'Cake Tin' in Wellington to see New Zealand qualify with a 1-0 victory through a 45th minute goal to Rory Fallon. New Zealand had made it to just their second World Cup.

The fairy tale for Smeltz continued in South Africa in 2010 when he became only the fourth New Zealander to score at a World Cup.

He did it in style against the title-holders, Italy, at Mbombela Stadium in Nelspruit. Smeltz scored in the seventh minute to put the All Whites in front. Italy equalised through a penalty later in the first half and the match ended in a 1-1 draw. New Zealand were undefeated in their group with two more draws against Slovakia and Paraguay, only missing out on the second stage by one point – a far cry from their three World Cup losses in 1982.

Smeltz definitely felt the support from New Zealand and even from the Australian tourists over in South Africa.

"We were having a good run, no one sort of expected it. We had a few players from the A-League at the World Cup. It felt like we had Australia behind us as well which was nice."

Smeltz would play at three Confederation Cups in 2003, 2009 and 2017. His international goals would come against countries such as Chile, Wales, Serbia and Italy twice. He won 58 caps for the All Whites and is second to only another Trans-Tasman legend, Vaughan Coveny, in goals scored with 24.

The list of personal honours for Smeltz is vast.

He had a prolific domestic career in the A-League. He played 190 games with Wellington Phoenix, Perth Glory, Sydney FC, and Gold Coast United for 92 goals. He won the Johnny Warren Medal for player of the season in 2008-09, and twice won the Golden Boot Award; first with Wellington Phoenix in 2008-09 and again with Gold Coast United in 2009-10. He also made the Professional Footballers Association Team of the Decade (2005-2015).

Given his resume and goal scoring nous, if he had stayed eligible for Australia there is no doubt he would have played for the Socceroos.

"There's so many boys that managed to get the odd cap for the Socceroos. A lot of people say to me *'You definitely would have played for Australia'*, but it wasn't to be."

"I would never change anything, it was a decision I made at the time, it was one I was excited about. The things I got to do!"

"As a kid it's something you dream about. I got to fulfill many childhood dreams by taking that path (with New Zealand)"

Just as Australia was needing a striker of Smeltz's calibre, he was scoring goals for New Zealand.

* * *

Christian 'Bobo' Vieri represented Italy with distinction, becoming a leading goal scorer in the Serie A and La Liga, playing for the likes of Juventus, Inter Milan and Atletico Madrid.

Yet he learned his football in western Sydney and his boyhood idol was the Test cricket captain Allan Border.

It all began in the late 1970s when the National Soccer League was starting in Australia.

Marconi's Frank Labbozetta was the manager of Club Marconi's soccer department and went to Italy to find a standout player for their team. With Club Marconi in Fairfield being an Italian-backed club they wanted someone who had played Serie A or with the Italian national team to lead their NSL side.

They managed to get in touch with Roberto Vieri, a fine domestic footballer who had played with Fiorentina, Prato, Sampdoria, Roma, Juventus and Bologna as well as games with Italy B. They convinced him to come to Australia for a short spell of three games in 1978. As club stalwart Tony Labbozetta put it:

"We brought him back for a season 1979. That's the year that we first won the championship. Roberto was the mastermind of the midfield that produced the goods for our strikers. That was the year that Roberto was at his peak."

Roberto's time in Australia was quite fruitful for him and his young family. Young son Christian would grow and develop here, as would daughter Veronica and later their second son Massimiliano (Max) who would be born in Sydney.

Having moved to Sydney at such a young age, Christian Vieri's earliest memories are not of Italy, but of western Sydney and are in English.

He became great family friends with the Labbozetta children, Attilio and Filomena, and he spent his summers outside becoming friends with children of all different backgrounds.

As a child, Vieri loved playing on the street, riding bikes and playing cricket. He loved athletics and he was always playing street cricket outside idolising Australian cricket captain and fellow leftie Allan Border. Football was never high on the agenda for Vieri until around the age of 14 when playing at Marconi.

Primarily used as a defender, Vieri wasn't enjoying his football and suggested to his coach that he should play as a forward. At the end of that first season in attack, he had scored 18 goals and his love and passion for football was beginning.

After that goal scoring season, Vieri was called into the age group above him to play in the finals. The team included former Socceroo captain Paul Okon, who is generally regarded as one of the most complete players ever produced by Australia, and was coached by Paul's father, Klaus.

Despite being the smallest player on the park, Vieri came off the bench and scored in a semi-final. Childhood friend Attilio Labbozetta remembers him playing in this game.

"I never forget there was a game for Under 17s and he was on the bench. He came on and scored a bomb from about 30 yards! Playing years above his age level! You see that and you know he's pretty special!"

According to Okon, there wasn't anything that stood out about his teammate.

"Back then I didn't think he would have gone to achieve what he achieved. I remember when he was playing up he scored some goals with us. That was always something he did pretty easily which, of course, is what he went on to do at the highest level."

That Marconi junior side would win the title. At the end of the season a trial in Italy was organised for both Okon and Vieri.

The boys went to Prato in Tuscany and stayed with Vieri's grandfather. Despite staying with relatives, Vieri was homesick for Sydney. The two *'Australian'* boys trialled with Prato but were given empty promises, nothing eventuated from that trip.

Okon returned home to Australia whilst Vieri decided to stay with his grandfather and wait for another trial somewhere else.

Soon enough, another local club in Santa Lucia asked Vieri to trial. Vieri scored easily at this level, but he still missed Australia and his family. He was constantly crying from homesickness. It became so bad that his father had to come to Prato to tell him *'If it's too hard for you, you best come back to Australia'*.

According to Vieri in his biography *Chiamatemi Bomber*, his grandfather saw some talent and persisted *"Bobo you have to stay in Italy. Here you can succeed. Italy is Italy. In Australia you won't go far. Who rates Australian football?"*

But Prato wasn't home for Vieri and, as an Australian, he wanted to continue his life in Sydney, so he returned home to Australia and his family.

However, on return to Sydney his grandfather's words echoed in his head and after some time reflecting, Vieri told his parents that he wanted to go back to Italy. They told him that if he wanted to go they would not be paying for the ticket.

Instead, the suburban club Santa Lucia paid for his ticket and he returned. Constantly scoring goals he was noticed by Prato, who then recruited him to their youth team. He performed there too and was then spotted by Serie A club Torino.

Tony Labbozetta reflects on Vieri's youth career in Italy.

"From Prato he was then picked up by Rosario Rampanti a very close friend of his dad who was the coach of Torino. From there he was nurtured into a player of reasonable standing and his left foot started to become recognised. From there he went to Venezia and then of course he was picked for the Italian national Under 21s by the father of Paolo Maldini (Cesare Maldini)."

Soon after, Vieri was playing for the Italian Under 21 side that won the Euro title. The Under 21 coach Maldini would take on the national team job in 1997 and through injuries in the senior team and on the back of his performances with the youth team, Vieri would be handed his first cap.

"When the Italian national coach resigned, Cesare Maldini took over for three matches. In these games he had to play (Christian). He had no strikers because the two strikers he had were injured," Tony Labbozetta recalls.

"So he called upon Christian, knowing that he had worked for him in the Under 21s and he did well. That was the break that Christian got."

Working his way in club football with Atalanta and then Juventus, Vieri would join Spanish giants Atletico Madrid for one season prior to the 1998 World Cup, winning the Pichichi Trophy for La Liga's top goal scorer. His transfer to Spain was almost double what Juventus had offered him to stay.

Vieri would go to the World Cup in France 1998, scoring five goals and attracting headlines across the world, including Australia. His interviews in English showcased a broad Australian accent straight out of western Sydney.

After the World Cup, Vieri would leave Atletico Madrid and return to Italy.

In a quirk of fate in 1998-99 Vieri and Paul Okon would be teammates again, in the Serie A with Lazio. A couple of boys from the Marconi juniors mixing it in Europe's elite. According to Okon he was clearly the number one Italian striker, scoring regularly.

After one season with Lazio, Vieri moved to Inter Milan for a world record transfer fee at the time. He would play with Inter more than any other Italian club, tallying 143 games and 103 goals.

During this stint he went to another World Cup with Italy in 2002, this time scoring another four goals. His goal scoring ability on the world stage was never in question.

Unfortunately for Vieri when Italy won the World Cup in 2006, he wasn't part of the squad, although it wasn't from lack of trying.

Attilio Labbozetta says that he left AC Milan in 2005 to try to make the squad.

"He went from Milan to Monaco because he wanted to go to the World Cup. He wasn't getting a lot of game time at Milan, so in his head he wanted to play more so he had a chance to go to the World Cup. Then he hurt his knee.

"He missed the 2006 World Cup and that hurt him. He won many trophies but nothing as significant as the World Cup. That was always one of his biggest let downs."

* * *

The Vieri name is strong in Australian football for other reasons.

As well as father Roberto playing in the National Soccer League, younger brother Max played for the Socceroos on six occasions. Australian-born Max was called into the Australian squad from Serie B, 12 years after his family had returned to live in Australia.

Max Vieri is another case of what might have been for Australia as he was rated higher as a junior by those at Marconi who knew them both.

"Max was probably the better footballer in terms of ability. Christian always had this desire to score and that stayed with him. A real desire, that hunger to try and succeed and score," says Okon.

"The comments from Roberto and several others who saw him play was that they expected Max to be the better player. He was more technically gifted and they did not expect that Christian would make it at the level that he did," adds Tony Labbozetta.

Max would be the first Australian to have a brother play for another country. He would later be joined by the Cahills and the Dengs (see Chapter 10 *Lost Socceroos Short Stories*) as brothers who have represented different countries.

* * *

Most Italian-Australians reflect on Christian Vieri's career with great pride. His ascent is quite amazing considering his humble football beginnings in western Sydney.

It is fair to say he couldn't have made it without his Australian background, yet he wouldn't have made it to the levels he did had he stayed in Australia.

Vieri's athleticism, competitiveness and physicality was undoubtedly born in Australia, but the discipline, technicality and coaching completed him in Italy. According to Attilio Labbozzetta, the physicality of Vieri was an Australian trait.

"I never saw him stage or dive. I mean if he got knocked over, he got knocked over. He was always strong in that way. If you look at all the goals he scored, he is just a really strong striker. You don't see many Italian players like that."

Christian Vieri was possibly the best striker of his era. He played in the best league at the time; he was the most expensive player in the world for a period; and scored nine goals in two World Cup appearances.

What an amazing career this boy from western Sydney had.

6
Australia's taxpayer funded stars – Seric, Ergic and Simunic

The golden generation of Australian footballers were on display in the 2006 World Cup, with 11 members of the 23-man Australian squad having spent time at the Australian Institute of Sport in Canberra. John Aloisi, Mark Bresciano, Brett Emerton, Josh Kennedy, Mark Milligan, Craig Moore, Lucas Neill, Josip Skoko, Mile Sterjovski, Mark Viduka and Luke Wilkshire were developed and honed as juniors within our government funded sports program.

However, at the 2006 World Cup there were 14 footballers in total who had spent time at the AIS. In addition to Australia's 11, Croatia had Ante Seric and Joe Simunic, whilst Serbia and Montenegro had Ivan Ergic.

How does it happen, that a taxpayer funded junior elite level program would produce players that would turn out for other countries? It is probably a consequence of a combination of Australia's culturally diverse population, as well as the Australian game and the administration at the time.

In the aftermath of Australia failing to clinch a spot at the 1998 World Cup in France, following the disastrous draw in the play-off match against Iran at the MCG, the Socceroos agreed to play Croatia in an out-of-season friendly in Zagreb to help prepare the Croatians for their first World Cup since gaining independence.

In what was Terry Venables final game as coach of Australia, the Socceroos picked a squad of mainly European based players and included a young left back from Hajduk Split to make his debut, Anthony Seric. The Croatian football association picked a side full of fit players ready to take on the world at France and included a young left back from Hajduk Split to make his debut, Anthony Seric.

Here was the almost comical situation where the same player was picked in squads for both countries to make their debut in the same game.

Ante 'Anthony' Seric was born in Sydney to Croatian parents and was brought to the AIS by Ron Smith. Smith had been involved in Australian football since the early 1970s and was heading up the program at the time.

"I brought Ante in. My last intake included lads like Mile Sterjovski Vince Grella, Brett Emerton, Simon Colosimo, Eddy Bosnar and Ante Seric. So that was quite a good squad of players, a number of whom went on to play for the Socceroos."

Smith had left the AIS to coach in Malaysia and former Socceroo defender Steve 'Rocky' O'Connor took over the program at the AIS. He remembers Seric and the process of identifying talent.

"Ante Seric was a good player who did well at the nationals, because the system in those days was, we had the state academies and of course the national youth league. Players from the state teams played in the national championships.

"We'd get a good vision of which players were around. You'd get to see most of the players in terms of their quality.

"Then you'd try and make your selections based on that, a bit of testing in terms of their pace, and look at what sort of positions they might be best suited to.

"We were looking at Ante mainly as a full back, but he could have been versatile. He was fairly quick, good engine, decent technically and a leftie."

Seric certainly had some ability as a teenager and he attracted the attention of Croatian powerhouse Hajduk Split, asking him to come for a trial as an 18-year old.

O'Connor knew they were going to lose him, when Seric approached him asking to head abroad and trial with Split.

"He came up to me early on at the AIS and asked could he go to Croatia for trials. I laughed it off straight away and thought he's not going to come back.

"I remember having him up in the office and I said '*Mate, you can go for trials. I can't stop you, make sure you come back and do your time here,*' and I pointed out a number of other players who had gone through the program and then gone on to play for top leagues overseas and things like that.

"It's not like we don't develop players that go and play in the top leagues, because we do that consistently.

"In the end, I couldn't stop him. He could just go anyway if he wanted to. We sort of did it on the proviso that he come back. But he never came back."

Seric was in Croatia and the newly independent nation was developing a scouting network to ensure that all talent that was Croatian or of Croatian heritage was included in their national setup.

Seric was confused and so he reached out to Ron Smith, the first talent identifier that brought him in to the AIS. Smith remembers the conversation.

"He rang me once and said: '*Look I've got this dilemma, what do you think I should do?*" and I said "*If you're undecided about where you want to play, I know the opportunity to do something right now, is very hard to resist, but it depends where you think you might finish up and where you want to play.*

"There is no guarantee that you will get picked to play for Australia but if Croatia is giving you an opportunity, they want to lock you in."

Locking-in players was an approach most countries were taking, with dual eligibility a real threat in modern international football. Australia was not immune to this approach ether with Harry Kewell debuting at 17, and Eddie Thomson handed an 18-year old Lucas Neill a cap to ensure he knew he was in their long term thinking as well.

According to O'Connor, there wasn't a lot else they could have done with Seric.

"We did our best to talk to the players and get them on side, but you can't always win."

History will show that Seric chose Croatia and the Australian football media was outraged. Here was a player, born in Sydney, who was selected for the taxpayer funded Australian Institute of Sport, choosing to snub the land that gave them his football opportunities.

Matthew Hall was the only Australian journalist in Croatia for Seric's debut, and what he remembers the most about the game, despite the drubbing, was Seric's first touch.

Seric came on as a first half substitute in the 40th minute. The first time he received the ball, he was met by Kevin Muscat, who enforced a 'Kevin Muscat tackle' on him.

Seric would have the last laugh as Croatia defeated the Socceroos, 7-0.

Seric's decision to play for Croatia would see him earn a Bronze Medal from the 1998 World Cup, as well as form part of their 2002 and 2006 World Cup squads, quite an achievement despite not seeing any game time in the three tournaments.

He would leave Hajduk Split after 33 games and join Hellas Verona in Italy's Serie A, famously featuring in Tim Parks storied 2002 book *A Season with Verona*. He played Serie A football with Verona, Brescia, Parma and Lazio, as well as stints in Greece, a return to Hajduk Split and in Turkey. He finished his professional career in Portugal in 2014.

* * *

Ivan Ergic was a 15-year old refugee when he and his parents migrated to Carnarvon in the mid 1990s, nine hours north of Perth in Western Australia.

Escaping the troubles of Serbia at the time, the family spent time in Croatia before joining relatives who were growers on the banana plantations. Ergic describes it as a typical refugee story, but something he really didn't want to do.

"I must say I wasn't delighted by the idea. I was 15 and already established as a potential young player. I knew something about Australia, I knew that soccer isn't one of the major sports and that was very disappointing thing for me.

"But we had no choice. Serbia at the time was a lot of trouble, and when my parents said we were moving I couldn't say too much."

Moving to Carnarvon from the Balkans was quite the cultural shock for Ergic.

As refugees it also meant starting from the bottom as his parents had to work in the fields and factories to try and restart their life in Australia. Socially it would be a struggle as well, but things moved quickly for Ergic, thanks to a local police sergeant who saw him playing football.

"He saw me play in the local Carnarvon league. He called some people in Perth and I went for a trial and from then on I played for the state team, Western Australia. They contacted someone in Canberra at the AIS and I went there for a trial and from then on things started to move pretty quickly."

Steve O'Connor remembers how Ergic came onto the AIS radar.

"Someone rang me from Perth and said there is this guy playing a little bit in Carnarvon, he's a good player. So we pulled him over to have a look at him and he had trials with us. He was clearly a decent player so we brought him in."

Ergic had only been one year in Carnarvon when he moved to Canberra, aged 16.

Given Ergic's refugee status, getting him eligible for the AIS was easy given their connections in Canberra.

"We had to get him naturalized. You couldn't get an AIS scholarship in those days unless you went through the naturalisation process. We got him through as fast as we could with contacts through the Government that the AIS obviously had. We got him fast tracked, he was an outstanding prospect there is no doubt about that."

With Ante Seric's decision to play for Croatia still fresh in the mind of the AIS administrators, Ergic was also made to sign a waiver with the AIS that he would not play for another country within three years.

O'Connor remembers a conversation he had with Ergic.

"He promised me he'd play for Australia if he got to that level."

Ergic looks back at his time in Canberra with fondness.

"The AIS was the best time of my life.

"All the friendships. It covers you first going out, your first drink, your first love. All these kinds of things were really happy for me there. The friendships though, when you live with twenty other 16-year-old's, you can imagine what kind of atmosphere that must have been."

Given his ability, and the happiness he felt at the AIS, it was every chance that Ergic would play for the Socceroos.

"His dribbling ability was extraordinary, and he was quick. He was very talented. The type of player who could take on three or four players and beat them with the ball. He had that ability to entice players in, with his touch, and then go around them," recalls O'Connor.

"He had this ability to dribble off the toe, which is dribbling the ball out in front of you more. You tend to do it more in open spaces but he could do it practically anywhere on the field. Lead with it out in front of him and have that touch where he enticed people in. They would come in to have a bite and they think they'd have it, and then he'd whisk it around them. That was an unusual talent, I hadn't seen the ability to do it that way for a long time."

Ergic and his close mate Ljubo Milicevic signed for Perth Glory straight out of the AIS, and played for them in the halcyon era of Perth Glory, starring in Perth's fourth season in the National Soccer League.

Ergic's 23 games at Perth Glory were outstanding. He was one of the best players in the National Soccer League, winning the Under 21 Young Player of the Year. In 2016, 20 years after Perth Glory was formed, Ergic was voted into the best ever Perth Glory XI in their history.

Such was Ergic's dominance he was signed by Italian giants Juventus on a 50-50 deal with Swiss club Basel.

Here was a player who less than five years earlier had moved to the backblocks of Carnarvon as a refugee from Serbia, now playing top flight football in Switzerland.

The deal saw him go straight to Basel, where he would potentially develop in the Swiss League, and then Juventus could take him to the Serie A.

Going from the national spotlight to playing in Europe, must have attracted the attention of the Australian selectors. Not so much according to Ergic.

"I remember there was always talk in Australia that I should be capped for Australia. At that time there was this whole philosophy we should get this player before he decides to play for another country. It's a big issue in Europe but at the time it was a speculative thing.

"There was some talk at the time while I was at Perth to get a call up for the national team, but it never happened. Nobody called me."

But Ergic wasn't worried about the Socceroos as he had achieved his aim of getting back to Europe with his football.

"We all dreamed of playing in Europe. For me it was the ultimate to come back where a football culture is. I was 18 or 19, it was surreal for me at the time. I played a really good season in Perth and was impressed with all the attention and I seized the moment. I thought about staying with Perth another year, but when you have an offer from a giant you cannot wait for too long."

Not long after arriving in Switzerland, it wasn't long before the scouts from then Yugoslavia were in touch with Ergic.

"As soon as I came to Basel, they contacted me straight away. I remember there were some other players that were born in Switzerland and elsewhere.

"At the time the federation had a policy of getting players that had links to Serbia (then Yugoslavia)."

By Ergic's second season at Basel, the team had qualified for the Champions League and he was playing some really good football.

"Then I got sick and I didn't play for two years."

Ergic suffered from depression and had a real struggle in regaining his health. Even today, he tends to divide his career into two, before his illness and after.

"I spent a lot of time with my psychiatrist, you know reflecting.

"Then I got a call-up for the World Cup, it was a surprise call-up for me. I didn't get a call-up when I was playing really good football. It was a time when I was coming back from my illness and then I got a call-up.

"For me, it would have been better much earlier."

Ergic would feature at the 2006 World Cup, coming off the bench for Serbia and Montenegro in a 6-0 loss to Argentina and playing against the Ivory Coast in a 3-2 loss.

"It was a bit ambiguous for me, the whole feeling. I hadn't played the qualifications, then I told the coaches that maybe it's not fair that I go to the World Cup without having played all these games. Of course there were some players who didn't get chosen who had been playing.

"I felt like a bit of an alien out there. Also we didn't play the best world cup."

With allegiances to both Australia and the former Yugoslavia, Ergic wasn't given the choice of who to play for with Australia not having approached him.

Ergic's decision to play for Serbia and Montenegro was for family and loyalty.

"My grandparents and all my friends lived there. I was born there. The country had been devastated from all the wars. I felt obliged as a person to do something for that country. It really was romantic patriotism, really nothing else.

"You are part of something big and you are playing for that country.

"In time it faded away. You know, the pride in the national team, and wearing the jersey and all that. It didn't have that lustre anymore.

"In the background there was this excessive nationalism that really disturbed me."

Since retiring from football, Ergic divides his time between Serbia and Switzerland.

Decisions on which country to play for is more of an issue in Switzerland than it ever was in Australia.

"People talk about sports bringing people together. I think it divides them more, especially when you see players who have to decide which country to play for.

"A lot of young players have to decide to play for Switzerland or Serbia and don't know what to do. There is the commercial aspect too. Is it going to bring more added value to the player in the market if he plays for one country over another country?"

Although his time with the national team was after his illness, Ergic felt obliged to help out Serbia.

"I believe I would have enjoyed much better status and better treatment in Australia than I did in Serbia. Despite all of that I decided to play for Yugoslavia."

Ergic would play over 200 games with Basel in Switzerland before a brief switch to

Turkey, winning the league with Bursaspor and playing Champions League again. He was capped 11 times at international level.

* * *

One of Australia's most famous games was against Croatia in the 2006 World Cup. Croatia needed a win to progress out of the group stage, the Socceroos only a draw.

During the game, Croatia's tough defender Joe Simunic received a yellow card in the 61st minute for body checking Harry Kewell.

Kewell would score the equaliser in the 78th minute to make the game 2-2, and in the time that followed the match would descend into farce.

Croatia's Dario Simic would earn his second yellow in the 85th minute and was sent off.

Brett Emerton received his second yellow in the 87th minute and was sent off.

Well into injury time, Joe Simunic fouled Josh Kennedy and received his second yellow card.

What should have been an automatic send off and red card didn't turn out that way.

English referee Graham Poll has stated in his book *Seeing Red* that he was confused by Simunic's Australian accent and marked the second yellow in his book against number 3 of Australia.

In sheer frustration and disappointment at the 2-2 draw that saw Australia progress to the second round, Simunic gave the referee a piece of his mind. For the spray, he was given his third yellow card and finally a red.

As ESPN commentator Tommy Smyth put it during their commentary of the game. *"How can you get that many cards? Unless it's Christmas time."*

That Simunic never received a yellow for his close checking of Socceroos captain Mark Viduka is probably the biggest mystery of the game.

It is typical of Croatian history that so many people left Croatia looking for a better life. Joe Simunic's parents did the same in moving to Australia, where Josip (Joe) was born in 1978 in Canberra.

Like many new arrivals to Australia, the Croatian community wanted to develop their own recognised identity. They opened churches, Croatian schools and football clubs. A six-year old Simunic joined Canberra Croatia Soccer Club, now known as Canberra Football Club.

His talent as a junior was instantly noticeable and, even as a 12-year old, opposition parents would remark to Simunic's father '*Your son will grow up to play for Australia one day*'. Simunic senior's reply was '*No, he will play for Croatia*'.

Ron Smith saw Simunic's talent whilst he was working at the AIS. With Simunic living in the nearby suburb of Kaleen, he got him into the Australian Institute of Sport early. He was training with the older boys to assist his development.

Smith believes when Eddie Thomson selected his side for the 1996 Atlanta Olympics and excluded Simunic, that might have been the catalyst for him to opt for Croatia. Given Simunic's age he could have made the 2000 Olympics side, which was one of the reasons that Eddie Thomson left him out as Smith recalls.

"I've had a conversation with Joe about this. He said to me "*Ronnie, when Eddie left me out of the squad, I was absolutely gutted, I wanted to play, I felt I was good enough and I was ready to play.*" Then Eddie said 'Well because we've got other players, who are good players, they might not be quite of Joe's calibre, but we can save him for the next one.'"

Smith believes that Simunic was more than good enough for that Atlanta squad, even though he was only 18.

Such was Simunic's talent that Socceroo Hayden Foxe credits his football knowledge to playing alongside Simunic, according to their AIS coach Steve O'Connor

"Hayden used to say "*I just watch and learn from Josip,*" because Joe played in the midfield at the time and Hayden was a defender. He (Simunic) was such an extraordinary talent that we missed out on."

In fact, both Simunic and Foxe went from the AIS to trial with Ajax Amsterdam. Foxe signed-on but the more highly rated Simunic missing out because he didn't score as well in the fitness tests.

Smith then realised that Simunic's tank may not be suitable for a high-level role in the midfield. His pace and height were assets, so Smith transitioned Simunic into probably the best defender this country has produced.

Smith told Simunic that as a defender he could no longer nutmeg opponents. Much later, Simunic told Smith on a trip home to Canberra after playing in Europe, that he remembered Smith's advice and now only nutmegs forwards when his team is 2-0 up.

After the AIS, Simunic joined Melbourne Croatia in the National Soccer League. He played briefly with Mark Viduka and won the title in 1995-96 as a teenager. His standout form as a youngster in defence saw him immediately sign a three-year deal with Hamburg in the German Bundesliga.

Always on an upward trajectory, according to Smith this was the first time that Simunic's career began to stall, with injury cruelling his time at Hamburg.

"In that three-year period I think he played about nine games. He broke his fifth metatarsal five times and didn't play football for nearly three years. He would recover, get back to training, play one or two games then break it again. Hamburg didn't renew his contract, because they thought what's the point.

"Joe is often asked why he didn't you play for Australia. In conversations I had with him, he said for a long time there he didn't know if he was ever going to be able to play football, let alone who he was going to play international football for."

After his injury, Simunic signed with Hertha Berlin and began to establish himself as a *bona fide* European player. It was here that Croatia came calling.

According to Steve O'Connor, it's fortunate for Australia that we didn't lose other players to Croatia.

"They had good contacts, we knew that was going on, but it's hard to stop. I mean you say to players that we've brought you in and worked with you and given you this opportunity so we want you to play for Australia. Some did like Mark Viduka.

"I remember walking Mark to the dining room and saying *"Mate don't you go and play for bloody Croatia"*. It wasn't as if we didn't broach it with the players; we certainly spoke openly about it.

"Sometimes the parents with Croatian backgrounds were very pro-Croatia so there was a lot of pressure on some of them. I'm sure there was on Mark as well when they came calling."

Ned Zelic is one of the best credentialed Socceroos from Canberra and is also of Croatian descent.

Like Simunic, Zelic also played for Canberra Football Club. He wasn't faced with a choice when he debuted for Australia, as Croatia hadn't yet gained independence. He doesn't begrudge Simunic's choice, and doesn't think Australian players do either.

"I obviously knew Joe was a supremely talented player and that he was going to go on to big things. I never expected him to have to make that decision to play for Croatia. That's where it came down to everyone's personal choice. Obviously in the back of the mind of players is '*What's better for my career?*'

"If you look at Joe he played at World Cups and he played at European Championships. Playing for Croatia worked out extremely well for him. Every year you had massive, meaningful games.

"A lot of people would have an issue with that. From a player's perspective I can perfectly understand the decision he made. I guess everyone's different and thinks about it differently.

"All Croats that have grown up here have a strong link to Croatia. But there are quite of few of us as well who think about it differently. This is the place I was born, I grew up here, I respect the country greatly. Everyone is different."

There is no denying that a country that was going to consistently qualify for World Cups would always beat a country that at that stage had only qualified for one. Smith recalls.

"I remember Joe saying to me that the fact that he was by then playing in Europe, it was easy to make the decision. We hadn't qualified for the World Cup and they had.

"And he was asked: *'Do you want to play in the World Cup?'* I mean how many people would knock that back?"

Simunic forged a formidable career in Europe. He played Champions League with

Hertha Berlin and Dinamo Zagreb. He went to two World Cups and three European Championships in a career that saw him capped over 100 times for Croatia. Given those early years in Germany, his resurrected career is remarkable according to Smith.

"His whole career was in jeopardy, considerable jeopardy for some years. When you consider how much football he missed, to play 105 games for Croatia was quite an achievement. It could have been a hell of a lot more."

Simunic lined up against Australia only once in his career, in that famous match at the 2006 World Cup.

He was openly booed by the Australian fans, according to Joey Didulica who was sitting on the bench. It was more like the booing players get when they change clubs within a league.

"It was Aussie humour, not malicious or anything, more in a jocular manner."

Simunic started the game, and fellow Australian born players, Joey Diduclica and Ante Seric, were on the bench.

As well as the 13 players from the AIS in the game, almost one-third of the Socceroos squad had Croatian heritage.

Watching replays of the game, Simunic clashed with Mark Viduka often. His defensive efforts restricted the Aussie talisman, but he was unable to stop the Socceroos getting the draw they needed.

Simunic's playing record should stand up as part of Australia's golden generation.

100 caps for Croatia, European Championships, World Cups, Champions League and playing over 200 games in the Bundesliga. It tends to be forgotten in Australia because he chose to play for Croatia.

Would he have made a difference with the Socceroos at the 2006 World Cup?

Journalist Michael Lynch wrote in the Fairfax press in 2015 that it is fascinating to think how a back four with the younger and mobile Lucas Neill playing at right-back with Simunic and Craig Moore in the middle and Ante Seric at left-back would have fared.

Maybe they would have overcome Italy in the Round of 16. We will never know.

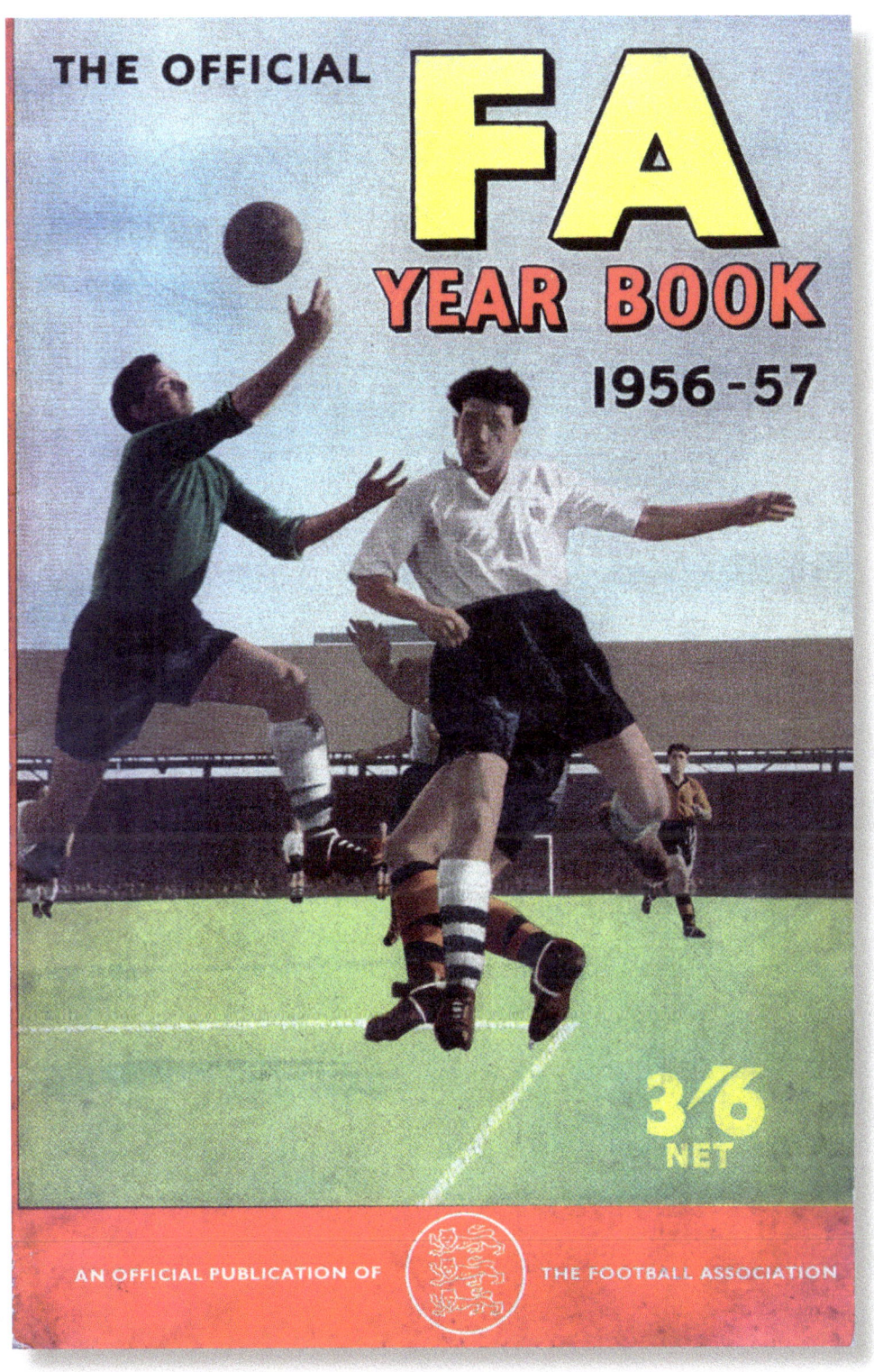

Ken Grieves, goalkeeper for Bolton Wanderers, gracing the cover of the FA Year Book 1956-57

Charlie Perkins playing for Adelaide Croatia, 1961

Christian Vieri and Paul Okon swap shirts after the Socceroos v World Stars match, Sydney 1999

Tim Cahill with Socceroos coach Frank Farina, 2005

Joey Didulica played four friendly internationals for Croatia between 2004 and 2006

Joe Simunic receives his third yellow card at the World Cup, Croatia v Australia, 2006

Shane Smeltz celebrates after scoring against Italy in the group match at Mbombela Stadium in Nelspruit at the South Africa World Cup, 2010

Dylan Tombides scoring for the Under 17 national team (the 'Joeys') against Côte d'Ivoire, 2011

Andrew Durante (#22) playing for New Zealand against Cristiano Ronaldo of Portugal at the Confederations Cup, 2017

7
DT38 – Dylan Tombides

Established in 1895 as Thames Ironworks and then renamed in 1900 as West Ham United, this is a football club that is one of the most famous clubs in the world, never more for the east London club than in the 1960s.

Winner of the FA Cup in 1964 and the European League Cup in 1965, the Hammers provided the backbone for the England side around that time with Geoff Hurst, Martin Peters and captain Bobby Moore.

Moore was their most famous son; good looking, immaculately dressed and the captain of both the Hammers and the 1966 England World Cup team. Moore is the man at the centre of England's greatest triumph, defeating West Germany for the World Cup trophy at Wembley Stadium, a game in which both of his West Ham teammates Hurst and Peters scored.

So revered is Bobby Moore that West Ham United retired his number six in 2008, 15 years after his passing. It was the first time the Hammers had retired a number.

In 2014 they retired a second number, this time it was number 38.

38 belonged to a young Australian taken too early by testicular cancer, his name was Dylan Tombides.

Dylan Tombides was born in Perth, Western Australia on 8 March, 1994, growing up in the northern suburbs. He was mad for football, playing for Wembley Downs, Stirling Lions and Perth Soccer Clubs, along with his brother Taylor with both showing promise.

His parents, Tracylee and Jim Tombides, were part of the casino industry and when the boys were in their early teens they were given the opportunity of setting up a casino in Macau. They packed up the whole family and headed overseas.

It's here that Tracy believes Tombides' football skills were refined.

"When we were in Macau the boys could play and train but they could never get involved in any actual games. So we decided to contact the Brazilian Soccer Schools over there. Every Friday, Jim, Dylan and Taylor or Dylan, Taylor and I would go to Hong Kong. We would train Friday night, they would play Saturday morning games against others kids their own age group and then we would go off on a Saturday afternoon and do a Coerver session, before we headed home to Macau on a Saturday night.

"The football in Macau was great for them. They played cage football on concrete surfaces. It was a bit of a free for all, but it got them the nitty-gritty style of games.

"They trained and played every day. You just got five mates together and rocked up to a caged game and joined in, anytime of the day, so it was always readily available."

This football mad lifestyle for the Tombides boys really paid-off, and before too long the large expatriate Portuguese community of Macau became aware of Dylan Tombides' talents and scouts were starting to know about him, so much so that he had offers to trial with Portugal football powerhouse clubs Sporting Lisbon, Benfica and Porto.

Just before these trials, Tracy Tombides was in Perth and bumped into Mike Leigh, who is a big part of the junior football community in Perth, working as a scout for West Ham United. Tracy Tombides told Leigh of Dylan's upcoming trial in Portugal.

Leigh told Tracy Tombides that he was going to West Ham in August and he requested that Dylan Tombides go to West Ham first, before he went to Portugal to trial.

Tracy agreed.

"So that's what we did. We went to West Ham in August instead of going to Portugal. I had the opportunity to move to London with work, so it was a good fit."

When Tombides arrived at West Ham as a 14-year old, it was the school holidays, so he had to join the older kids and play and train with the Under 18s. According to Tracy he really held his own.

The Academy Director, Tony Carr, liked him and when the Tombides family relocated to London, West Ham took Dylan and his brother Taylor.

Daniel Garb is a Western Australian journalist who was based in London for Fox Sports at this time.

"By the time he was taken in, he was already recognised as a big talent. You know what it's like in academy systems, you've got a number of players that are making up the numbers, as they have to fill up a squad," says Garb.

"When you're in a Premier League academy, it doesn't necessarily mean that much, even if you are Australian. A lot of kids are a part of Premier League academies and youth systems and not amount to anything, and that's nothing on them, it's just the way it goes. You have to stockpile a lot of players on your books.

"Dylan was certainly of the other variety, a top-class talent who was earmarked for the first team. There are only two or three players in every squad with that asterisk next to their name. He was a different breed and they treated him differently and from the age of 17 they thought '*This kid will play for us*;."

Tombides plied his trade with the West Ham youth teams, the Under 16s, Under 18s and the reserves.

But with the world at his feet, things changed dramatically for Tombides in 2011 when he found a lump on his testicle. He didn't say anything. Playing constant football, when he did experience some pain, he assumed it was all the exercise he was doing.

He eventually relented and saw a general practitioner and was misdiagnosed with having a benign cyst.

Tombides was told that people can live with these cysts, so he continued with his routine of football, football and more football.

On top of his game and feeling on top of the world, Tombides was selected to start on the bench for West Ham for the final game of the 2010-11 Premier League season against Sunderland.

If he was to get on the pitch, he would become the youngest Australian to play in the English Premier League, surpassing Harry Kewell who earned that honour for Leeds United in 1995 as a 17-year old. Alas he didn't get any minutes, and soon after, whilst still on that high, he travelled to Australia to join his Australian teammates for the Joeys in the Under 17 World Cup to be held in Mexico a month later.

Playing for the Joeys in this tournament, Tombides showed not only his talent on the pitch for scoring goals but he also showcased his big personality.

Playing against the Ivory Coast with scores level at 1-1, Tombides managed to change feet in the box, swivel and then score with his left boot in the 77th minute. It turned out to be the winning goal in a 2-1 result. In the midst of his goal celebrations, he ran to the camera, pulled out his shin guard and showed off his hand written message '*Happy Birthday Mum*' to the world.

So good was Tombides at this tournament, he was offered a five year contract from Nike.

Tombides played in all four games for the Joeys in that tournament. Australia was eliminated in the Round of 16 by Uzbekistan and after that game Tombides was selected to undertake a random drugs test.

The results of this test came back positive for a tumour and on his return to England, three months after his original medical consultation, he was diagnosed with testicular cancer and commenced chemotherapy immediatcly.

Being young and still feeling strong, Tombides tried to maintain his fitness, even when undergoing treatment.

But after treatment, the tumour metastasized. In 2012 he underwent the removal of his lymph nodes.

Once again, feeling in full health, he resumed training at West Ham.

Later that year on 25 September 2012, aged 18, Tombides made his first team debut for West Ham United in the League Cup (Capital One Cup). Playing Wigan Athletic, Tombides replaced Gary O'Neil in the 84th minute in what turned out to be a 4-1 loss at home.

Later in 2012 and again in 2013, Tombides had some major setbacks, requiring two stem cell transplants as well as having his liver resected. He continued to go in to

West Ham daily playing snooker and, in the words of the DT38 website, working on his banter.

In November 2013 his cancer had returned, but Tombides was intent on representing Australia in January 2014 playing for the Under 23s Asian Football Confederation tournament in Muscat, Oman. He had an intense three-week chemotherapy session beforehand in order to make the tournament.

He played for the Under 23s in all four games of the tournament against Kuwait, Iran and Japan, before the Olyroos lost their quarter-final to Saudi Arabia 2-1.

On his return to England, Tombides was told that his condition had become incurable. His condition deteriorated rapidly and he passed away three months later on 18 April 2014.

Following his tragic death at the age of 20, West Ham were at home to Crystal Palace.

His father Jim and brother Taylor took out his jersey with number 38 to the centre circle prior to the start of the game, in a moving tribute at Upton Park, home of the Hammers.

Garb was at this game and remembers.

"It was incredibly moving. The tribute at Upton Park was unbelievable. I did not expect that at all. As an Australian I was incredibly proud to see Australian flags with Dylan Tombides name emblazoned on them on the gates at Upton Park. It was just so moving. Then speaking with supporters and seeing supporters cry; for a player who had never played a Premier League game for the club, it was unbelievable really. So incredibly sad, Australian football needs to be very, very proud of that."

West Ham lost 1-0 to Crystal Palace on that day. The goal scorer for Palace was Socceroos captain Mile Jedinak.

Jedinak did not celebrate his goal in a mark of respect for his fellow Australian Tombides. Straight after the game he met the Tombides family, and immediately formed a strong bond and connection. The bond continues to this day, with Mile Jedinak a Patron for the DT38 foundation, along with Garb.

"I was asked by the family to approach Mile to see if he would help after they decided to set up the Dylan Tombides Foundation. I remember mentioning it to him and literally straight afterwards he called Tracy Tombides and said '*Whatever you want, I will do*'," recalls Garb of Jedinak's involvement.

"Mile has been an unbelievable help to the family since then. He has put forward financial help to the Foundation. He has become a friend and a confidante of the Tombides. He has helped with getting the Socceroos to get behind the Dylan Tombides Foundation before games, doing special tributes, things like that. He has been the shining light of that Foundation. I think he saw it as fate for him, because of his involvement in that game after Dylan's passing and also as an Australian abroad, being just so moved by the story."

Tombides' mother Tracy reflects on her relationship with Mile Jedinak and his entire family following Dylan's passing.

"We spend birthdays, Easter and Christmases holidays together as one big Australian family. It's special.

"He didn't know Dylan, but he knew of Dylan. He met him once when Dylan was a guest up in Scotland when Australia went up there to pay Scotland in 2012. Mile was part of the team then, he met Dylan, and he said to me that Dylan was well known through the Australian ranks as someone that was going to be pushed through. I mean, he can't do enough for the Foundation. His wife Natalie is lovely, his kids are great, it's a fun environment to be in."

Not long after his death, West Ham retired the number 38. According to Garb it was more to do with his personality than his potential ability.

"They did it because he's a special talent but also because he was a person who left a lasting impression on people at the football club. For someone to have their number retired having played one game for West Ham, and a League Cup game, just speaks volume for his potential and more so what he was as a person."

Tombides was the type of player the Socceroos were crying out for in the 2018 World Cup 2019 Asian Cup, where goals from open play only came in two of eight games.

According to Garb, the Socceroos had earmarked him as a player of note.

"Pure and simple we don't have the depth where we can afford to lose a talent like Dylan Tombides, simple as that. We don't have the amount of players where special talent comes along that we can cope with them not being there.

"It has hurt Australian football enormously, because we're sitting here talking about the lack of quality strikers and we lost one.

"We lost one who Ange Postecoglou earmarked leading into the 2014 World Cup. Ange is on the record as saying that *'I'm thinking seriously of taking Dylan Tombides to this World Cup, because we've got to get him into the system. He's just that good.'* That's the way he was thought of, and that's what he could have done for Australian football. It's a huge tragedy that his life was lost."

"You only have to speak to the coaches at West Ham who have seen hundreds and thousands of players come and go and fall by the wayside to know that he was the real deal.

"They don't persist with a player, who was as sick as Dylan was for years, unless they know he's the real deal.

"They were happy to keep Dylan on for years because they knew that he was Premier League quality, even after the illness that he had gone through. So that was the difference with him basically. He was, without a doubt, the player who would have spearheaded the Australian attack and would have been the household name in Australian football that the squad maybe lacks today."

Sam Allardyce is a big name in English football with an extensive managerial resume, he was in charge of West Ham when Dylan passed.

Garb spoke with him at the time.

"You could tell that Sam was heavily moved by Dylan's passing because not only is there a football loss here, but there's a personal loss, and they were very moved at West Ham, enormously, by Dylan's personality, the fact that he showed such incredible spirit.

"There are so many people who have had their footballing dreams taken away from them, slowly but surely, because of his illness would have been crestfallen and moody and downcast, and Dylan wasn't and the line that followed him around was '*He was the happiest kid in the world with cancer*'.

"He just had a smile on his face and fought hard, showing incredible spirit and resilience in a very positive way every time he went into the club and everyone at West Ham was moved by that enormously."

Tracy Tombides cannot speak more highly of West Ham United and what they have done since Tombides was there on their books. In 2019 the Academy of Football at West Ham named its education centre the Dylan Tombides Education Centre and the Academy's Player of the year award is also named after Tombides.

"West Ham rolls out the DT38 education to 25 schools. They've really taken on board the charity. At the very top of the stadium, is a place called the Academy Lounge. It's got every player that's ever graduated from the West Ham Academy like Rio and Anton Ferdinand, Frank Lampard, Joe Cole, Michael Carrick, Jermain Defoe, Glen Johnson, Mark Nobel, James Tomkins all these guys and they've got Dylan there.

"It's just wonderful, that it's how highly they thought of him, that he was someone that was destined for a Premier League life.

DT38 is the principal charity partner of West Ham United, along with the Bobby Moore Foundation.

In a strange coincidence, after Bobby Moore's passing from cancer in 1993 it was revealed that he had also suffered from testicular cancer in the 1963-64 season, having borne a growth for more than a year. History records that Moore missed some football through a routine groin operation. To his teammates, he told them he suffered from a "groin strain" trying to run it out and just get on with his football.

Once he did see a Urologist, a tumour was found and an orchidectomy was performed, the removal of Moore's testicle.

Both Bobby Moore and Dylan Tombides have statues to commemorate their lives, Moore's outside Wembley, Tombides' outside Perth Stadium.

The Moore statue depicts a man at the peak of his powers as captain of a World Cup winning side, foot on the ball. Tombides' statue reflects his personality and talent, the 'shin guard' moment with *'Happy Birthday Mum'* written on it in Australian colours for the Joeys.

The DT38 Foundation aims to promote awareness in testicular cancer. If detected early, the rates of survival are 95% and improving. If it wasn't for the initial misdiagnosis, Tombides could well have commenced treatment much earlier.

Awareness is the key and an early diagnosis is everything. If you're a male check yourself out, if you're a female, tell all the males in your life to check themselves.

As the DT38 Foundation says: delay is deadly, get educated.

8
Righting the wrongs – The Cahill Rule

Tim Cahill is Australia's greatest ever goal scorer with 50 international goals and has played the second most number of games for the Socceroos with 108.

He has gone to four World Cups and scored in three of those. He is always spoken about when the greatest ever Socceroos are discussed and had a habit of scoring goals on the biggest of big stages. But he did not play for Australia until he was 24 years of age because he was deemed ineligible to represent the Socceroos prior to that.

As a 14-year-old, Tim and his older brother Sean got a free trip to the home of their mother, Samoa. It was football-related, but they saw it as a chance to visit their sick grandmother.

Tim came on as a late substitute in an Under 20 game against New Zealand in a 3-0 loss. Little did Tim or the Cahills' realise that these few moments would tie him to Samoa for future senior international matches.

Whilst playing football with Millwall in the UK, Socceroos coach Frank Farina called Cahill into a camp in 1999 only to find out from FIFA that he was ineligible because of those few minutes for Samoa.

As far as Cahill was concerned he was an Australian, born in Sydney, grew up in Australia and he wanted to play for the Socceroos.

If the rules were to change for senior football, Cahill was also eligible for England through his father, and Ireland through his grandmother, with former Millwall and then Ireland manager Mick McCarthy showing some interest in Cahill for the 2002 World Cup.

Cahill put his allegiances in context in his book *Legacy*.

"You can't represent a country if you don't even know the national anthem."

So how did Cahill become a Socceroo?

According to Farina, who eventually gave Cahill his debut in 2004, it was because of journalist the late Michael Cockerill and the Socceroos part-time Operations Manager, Bonita Mersiades.

"I am not going to take credit for it, because the people that should take credit for it, and they deserve the credit, are Bonita and Mike, they lobbied and they lobbied," according to Farina.

Cockerill worked tirelessly in the media. He campaigned for the rules to change and for Cahill to be eligible to play senior football for Australia. According to Mersiades, Cahill's father was in contact as well, wanting him to play some form of international football.

"We certainly knew that Tim's Dad was keen for him to play somewhere internationally. I think he was eligible for Ireland, England and Australia and Tim's dad was in touch with all of those countries," Mersiades says.

"Mike championed the cause in the media and Frank met Tim and got to know him. Frank was very keen for him to play for Australia from when he was appointed coach in 1999."

Farina realised Cahill was passionate about representing Australia.

"I spoke to Timmy and I knew from the first time that he wanted to play for Australia. But we couldn't do anything because of the rules. There were a lot of other countries who were wanting the rules to change for players."

According to Farina that is when Mersiades began to campaign FIFA directly.

"She pushed it and pushed it, writing letters to FIFA and all this sort of stuff about changing rules," Farina says.

Mersiades sees it differently. "I only did what anyone would have done. That is, we looked at what the regulations were, we looked at what the rules were, and started to mount the case for why those rules needed changing. All I did was write."

Luckily for Australia, other countries were also wanting the rules adjusted.

"I believe there were some other countries at the time that were trying to make changes as well. I remember talking with someone at FIFA at the time and they said this has come up with other people as well. Clearly all we had knowledge of, or were interested in, at the time was Tim."

In 2003 FIFA changed the rules: players could be cleared to play for another country at senior level even if they had represented other countries at underage level.

The next game for the Socceroos in 2004 saw Cahill debut against South Africa in London under Farina, as a 24-year old.

"He came off the bench in London," Farina recalls. "Then the rest is history, I asked him to come to the Olympics. He was with Everton at the time, he came to the Olympic Games, and then mate, talk about a fucking skyrocket going off!

"He's amazing, he is the greatest Socceroo of all time!"

* * *

After missing out on the likes of Ante Seric and then Joe Simunic, the Cahill rule became the catalyst for Australia to change its scouting methods. Players who would slip through our grasp once upon a time became senior Socceroos.

More players followed who went on to represent the Australian national team, despite playing underage football somewhere else. These included Milos Degenek (Serbia), Apostolos Giannou (Greece), Jackson Irvine (Scotland), Neil Kilkenny (Ireland and England), Jamie Maclaren (Scotland), Brad Smith (England), Aleks Susnjar (Serbia) and Rhys Williams (Wales).

From 2014 to 2018 when Ange Postecoglou was in charge of the national team, these players would be recruited to the national team after playing underage football for other countries.

"Historically we missed out on a few good ones and I used to think that players should want to play for Australia and we shouldn't have to try and convince them. The nation went down that route for a little bit and even before I got the national team job I thought to myself that these guys have to make a pretty big decision at a young age. If they've made a decision we shouldn't rule them out playing; there wouldn't be any less significance for them to play for Australia just because they've played for another nation," says Postecoglou.

"When I got the national team job there were quite a few in that boat. I kind of made the point of reaching out to them and seeing what their attitude would be like. If they had a desire to play for the country we tried to cap them as soon as possible.

"A lot of people said we tied them in, but more so than tying them in, it gave them an allegiance to us. If they were going to develop over time, they were going to develop as Australian players."

Postecoglou's scouting methods went far and wide, using 62 players in his stint at the top. He looked at everyone.

"It was every Australian player, whether playing here or abroad. I don't know what that number would be up to, irrespective of the level they were playing, first team or reserves."

Postecoglou had Ante Milicic, one of his senior assistant coaches, base himself in Croatia. Milicic was able to keep a closer eye on the Socceroos pool of players by being closer geographically and in the same time zones.

"It's interesting there are so many players that we probably haven't even touched the surface. Players who we are not aware are eligible to play for Australia - you know they've left early or they have some kind of Australian heritage. A lot of the ones you get to is by design, but a lot is by luck as well. There is no real magic or straightforward formula.

"A lot of it is going out and speaking to people. I also speak to a lot of ex-players I played with, particularly in Europe. A lot of it is running into people. I often go to games and sit in areas where you can sense that the people aren't from that club and then you have little conversations, and when you say you're from Australia they might say do you know this player or that player, we had this player on trial."

According to Postecoglou the bush telegraph works in football too.

"Along the way you got information about guys with Australian links. You go down the track of seeing what their eligibility status was. For me, any player that was eligible to play for Australia was on our radar."

There is now software available for clubs and national teams that showcases players from all over the world, databases like Wyscout and InStat. These tools are all about sports performance analysis, looking at individual and team performances, player fitness and includes vision and game footage as well.

Milicic has a long history with this type of program, using Wyscout as the basis for establishing the Western Sydney Wanderers, when he worked as an Assistant Coach to Tony Popovic.

"I lived on Wyscout for a good six years, when I first come across to the Western Sydney Wanderers. We had to fill up to 23 players. There were players' names, agents, USBs with videos and then we got this Wyscout and you know what, I don't even want to know where he played, just give me his name. We would type in his name, we had this formula of the player's history, games played, positions played. It's crazy; it gets games from these remote areas, youth tournaments all around the world.

"Pop and I would go through and watch two to three games of pretty much every player that came across our desk, home and away, and then we would build a profile like that."

With distance always a factor when analysing Australian players, Milicic's use of these tools continued with the Socceroos when he was based in Europe.

"Ange wanted me to spend a year in Europe to monitor a lot closer and also to educate myself and that's what I did. Prior to that every couple of days I was downloading games and watching games, watching our players and its good because some of the things you can see on that Wyscout you can take into your Socceroos camp. Little things like in their club, where they are comfortable in standing on set pieces and what position they play in their club and their formation and how does that relate to the Socceroos.

"I watched a lot of players, but once you get on that Wyscout, now InStat, you sort of just go from one player, and you see another player, and then there is a link of players with similar profiles and in the end you could end up in any league in the world and at any club."

Fran Karacic is an interesting case in point. He had never set foot in Australia when he was called into the Australian World Cup squad for the 2018 World Cup.

Karacic was eligible because his father had an Australian passport, so how did the

Socceroos discover he was eligible? According to Milicic he had been on their radar for a while.

"We were looking at him for the Confederations Cup in 2017 in Russia. He was one that we were following. When you go on these platforms like Wyscout and Instat, you see the players' names and they used to put up flags of what country they are from.

"A lot of players do that so they can get registered in the country they are trying for and a lot of our boys do that too. Fran was one we came across and then we watched his games. He was young and versatile.

"I watched him a few times, Ange watched him a few times. Given I speak Croatian, I got in touch with Fran and introduced myself."

Despite playing eight games for Croatia's Under 21 side in 2017, FIFA cleared him to play for the Socceroos. Playing in Croatia with NK Lokomotiva, Fran was cut from the 26-man squad and didn't go to Russia. He is yet to debut for Australia.

It has become increasing prevalent that player agents are the ones making country's aware of the eligibility of their players. A player who has played for his national team can increase in value, and thus the agent's percentage can increase as well. The country that the player represents can also increase their club contracts. If you play for a European country, you will attract a higher salary than if you played for Australia. Milicic suggests that the agents are having an increased role in their players decisions.

"Look at Karacic. With no disrespect, if he plays for the Croatian national team, he has a different value then he would if playing for the Australian national team.

"Agents nowadays, they can influence players to some extent more than probably what coaches do. So that's the difference."

Postecoglou agrees.

"The agents see that if their guy plays international football the value of their player increases. A lot of agents saw it as a good career move."

Australia's modern scouting methods include basing coaches in the United Kingdom and on the continent, it's giving them access to extensive scouting software and it's being made aware of players eligibility through player agents, coaches and parents. Is it enough for Australia to compete in Asia and at World Cups? Are we giving ourselves every opportunity? Milicic thinks we might still be missing out.

"You get tipped off a few times. Often clubs will contact you or the federation, agents will as well, eager parents of young kids as well.

"I wish we had a network of ten people looking at it. Sometimes it's luck you know."

However, rather than being a good career move for players, most Australian fans still want the Socceroos to show some pride in the shirt. As a former player with the Socceroos, Postecoglou wanted the same.

"As the national team coach, you do want to see that they want to play for Australia. That's where it becomes a little tricky.

"It's a bit of a balancing act, you kind of want them to earn their spot in the national team and there is a school of thought that goes down that track. I always thought that, but at the same time I thought we had to be nimble in the way we did things."

Milicic thinks having an Australian coach helps with that mindset in getting the players who want to play for Australia and getting the best out of them but if they have a choice of countries it becomes a big decision.

"There is a different feeling let's be honest here. Especially the ones that have to make a decision when a couple of countries are chasing them. It's such a big decision and you've got to realise from a professional point of view and from a footballing point of view, if you are based in Europe and your club football is in Europe to make a commitment to the Australian national team with the travelling and the distance and the different confederations. It's a huge decision."

Postecoglou worked his magic on some players who will hopefully become stars of our game, famously picking Chris Ikonomidis straight from the Under 21 comp in Italy to play for the Socceroos.

Australia's modern scouting methods were on show prior to the 2018 World Cup when Aleksandar Susnjar debuted under Bert Van Marwijk in a friendly against Norway.

Susnjar is an interesting case in how he came to the attention of the Socceroos hierarchy, and showcases the modern approach. Postecoglou takes up the story.

"I got alerted from somebody in Perth, who told me there is this kid playing in the Czech Republic and he's eligible. I put him onto Ante's radar."

Susnjar was born in Perth to Serbian parents. He represented Serbia at Under 17 level but the football he was playing in Europe was in Lithuania, Slovakia, Romania and the Czech Republic, countries that weren't exactly front and centre when it came to coverage. Milicic picked him for the Under 23s once he was alerted.

The most unusual scouting according to Milicic was when the Socceroos played Greece in a couple of Australian based friendlies back in 2016. Postecoglou had recently convinced Apo Giannou to play for the Socceroos even though he had played in a senior friendly for Greece.

"That was a good one of Ange's with Giannou. When we were showing the (Socceroos) team footage, we had to make sure we didn't use the clip where we had Apo playing for Greece."

Another one under Postecoglou's reign was a player at Hibs in Scotland called Jason Cummings who they found out had some Australian links.

"Jason Cummings, who has some sort of Australian heritage and was doing quite well. So we would scout them a little bit, monitor them and then make decisions."

Cummings was selected and played for Scotland in 2017, but it was another 'Scottish' player at Hibs that would eventually join the Socceroos.

Martin Boyle came onto Australia's radar and he debuted for the Socceroos in 2018 under Graham Arnold. Here was a player who had never set foot in Australia until called upon to debut in Sydney. Of Scottish heritage, Boyle's father was born in Australia and held an Aussie passport, Arnold recounted the discovery on Fox Sports "The Back Page" in October 2018.

"I went to Hibs to look at Mark Milligan and Jamie Maclaren, and to meet their boss, and their boss, Neil Lennon said to me *'I shouldn't be telling you this, but you do know we have a player here whose father has an Australian passport?'*. I said *'Great we'll have him'*. I'll sign him up straight away, and I did."

Max Vieri held the unofficial record of not being in Australia for twelve years until his debut; this was eclipsed by Martin Boyle when he debuted age 25 in Sydney.

Just another example of Australian football trying to right the wrongs of the past.

9
Chasing higher honours – The Aussies who went another way

What about the Australians who didn't make the Socceroos. Would they have a chance elsewhere? We look at those who chose to chase higher honours with other nations.

Andrew Durante was playing for New Zealand's Wellington Phoenix in the A-League when he was called into a predominantly Australian-based Socceroos squad for an Asian Cup Qualifier against Indonesia in Brisbane in 2010.

Durante started the game on the bench and just after half time he was told to warm up as Mark Milligan was coming off with an injury. Instead, Milligan managed to play out the game.

"So I ran the whole half to warm up, but never ended up going on."

This was to be Durante's best and last chance to play for Australia.

The chance of international football presented itself again not long afterwards from his Wellington Phoenix club coach Ricki Herbert who was also the coach of the New Zealand national team, the All Whites. Durante recalls.

"My five years was coming up. Ricki said *'If you don't make the next Socceroos squad would you consider coming over to New Zealand and playing for us? We'd love to have you.*

"I was like *'We'll see when the next camps come out.'* Holger Osieck had just taken the job in charge of the Socceroos and I wasn't selected in his first squad. My five years was up and I was eligible to play for New Zealand. Ricki approached me again and I took up the opportunity."

The rivalry between Australia and New Zealand is well documented in other sports, but within football circles they are more like mates. New Zealand club sides were part of the old National Soccer League and they had teams in the A-League as well. So how did it feel for an Aussie, who had always dreamed of playing for the Socceroos, to suddenly feel like a Kiwi?

"It was a huge decision to switch allegiances. I didn't think I'd ever get a Socceroos cap. I was 30 when I changed over so I felt like I missed that opportunity to represent Australia, which is what I always wanted to do.

"I knew of the big rivalry between New Zealand and Australia, so I knew it was a big decision. I felt it was right as I had really set-up roots in New Zealand. My children were born there, we had really settled there, my wife was happy there, we had property there. I felt like I was a part of the New Zealand footballing culture and setup anyway."

As Durante was already playing with Wellington Phoenix it was quite a smooth transition. His club coach was the national coach and half of the New Zealand squad plied their trade with the Phoenix.

"I already knew all the players"

Durante officially became a New Zealand citizen in 2013, five years after joining the Phoenix. The next day he was named in the All White squad in a World Cup Qualifier against the Solomon Islands as part of the Brazil 2014 qualifying campaign.

New Zealand would win the Oceania group and then would face Mexico in a home and away play-off to reach the 2014 World Cup. The newly capped Durante would feature in both legs.

The All Whites were up against it after losing the first leg in Mexico City 5-1. They fared little better at home losing 4-2 and missed out on qualification. For Durante, the game in Mexico would become an amazing football experience.

"The atmosphere was just spine tingling. An incredible atmosphere that people in Australia or New Zealand wouldn't understand. You were there playing in front of so many of these crazy fans.

"The Azteca stadium has so much history. The noise of 100,000 people was incredible. I will never forget walking out for the national anthem, and you could feel the energy and the noise just going through your bones. It was rattling, the most intense atmosphere."

Durante's biggest year with the All Whites was in 2017.

The Oceania champions, New Zealand qualified for the Confederations Cup in Russia and Durante played in all three games against Russia, Mexico once again and Portugal. The Confederations Cup turned out to be a highlight of his international career.

"It was amazing. It was my first major tournament. I played some friendly games and a few World Cup Qualifiers, but to play against teams like Mexico, Portugal and Russia on a really big stage like the Confederations Cup was amazing.

"I got to play against Ronaldo! I have some photos of that. It was really special and just a great experience I had playing in that tournament."

Durante would also play in both legs of the final World Cup play-offs against Peru to quality for Russia 2018 - another money can't buy experience.

"No one in Rugby League or Rugby Union could ever experience something like that in their code. Football is a religion to them (Peru). It was passion. You could see how much qualifying for Russia meant to this country.

"They were letting off fireworks the night before our game. They were trying every trick in the book. They had fighter jets fly over our hotel the day before the game in Peru. Just tactics that wouldn't happen in other codes to unsettle players.

"It was awesome, I mean we were trying to sleep, but it showed how much passion and how desperate they were for their country to get through to the World Cup."

After playing a 0-0 draw at home, New Zealand lost the second leg in Lima 2-0 and missed qualification for the second consecutive World Cup.

Durante ended up with 24 caps for New Zealand and retired after the play-off loss to Peru. Later in the same year, he also become the first footballer to make 300 A-League appearances.

"I always wanted to play at the highest level and test myself to see how good I could be against some of the better players in international football. So that kind of made the decision to play for New Zealand a little bit easier."

* * *

Melbourne born and raised, Emmanuel 'Manny' Muscat played for over ten years in the A-League, 192 games in New Zealand with the Wellington Phoenix before returning home to Melbourne to play for Melbourne City and winning the FFA Cup in 2016.

"In football you never know what might happen, but I pretty much scripted what I wanted to do and it's worked out so well."

A registered builder playing part time football in the Victorian National Premier League with Green Gully, Muscat was recruited by Wellington Phoenix at the relatively old age of 23. In his first season at Wellington, Malta contacted the club asking him to be involved in their World Cup Qualifiers for South Africa 2010.

Manny's parents arrived in Australia from Malta around the ages of 19, and for Muscat the involvement in the Malta setup wasn't a complete shock for him.

"My parents have a couple of properties and holiday places in Malta. So we go back as much as we can."

* * *

Malta made quite a different approach to former Central Coast Mariners skipper John Hutchison.

Hutchison holds the record for the most combined NSL and A-League appearances with 394 games. Out of the blue one day he received an email from an innovative Maltese coach.

"I didn't actually know that I was eligible to play for Malta. I got a random email one day from their Head Coach, Dusan Fitzel. It asked if I was keen to play for Malta. I thought it was one of my mates mucking around."

Hutchison's Maltese heritage is from his grandparents on his mother's side, with the family name of Chircop.

His eligibility can be put down to the persistence of Hutchison's wife who did the required research. This included finding out the name of the boat on which his grandmother travelled to Australia.

"I'm too lazy to find those details out. I would have never gone through with it. My wife was the one who chased all the details on it. It just kind of bounced from there."

So after some Skype calls with the coach, he agreed to play for Malta.

He had never been to the country prior to his selection.

While Hutchison had forged a handy domestic career, the so-called 'golden generation' of the Socceroos prevented from being selected for the Australian side.

"I remember turning up to one Under 20 camp (Australia) and in similar positions to me were Jason Culina, Brett Emerton, Mile Sterjovski, Vince Grella and Mark Bresciano. I went home and Dad asked me how I went and I told him I was zero chance of ever getting selected.

"We had a decent midfield back then. I'm not bitter about never playing for Australia because at the time I wasn't good enough. I did make a few Socceroos camps and did all the training but never got a game.

"If I had known about the Maltese thing all along I probably would have done it earlier."

* * *

Hutchison and Muscat made their Malta debuts in the same game, a friendly against the Czech Republic before they were both selected for World Cup Qualifiers against Sweden. Having Muscat around really helped for Hutchison.

"It was just me and Musky at the time who were Australian-Maltese. The rest were from Malta or had left Malta to play in overseas leagues. It was nice to have someone in the same situation as me, because I never knew what to expect.

"I had never been to Malta. I didn't speak the language. Manny did speak the language and understood it, which helped."

For Muscat it was an easier transition.

"I roomed with Hutch every time we were together. Maltese people speak English quite fluently and it was quite easy for us, even for John, to understand and to communicate with the players and staff."

Playing in a World Cup qualifier against Sweden in Gothenburg, Muscat and

Hutchison found themselves facing a team that included Zlatan Ibrahimovic, for their first official cap.

They went down 4-0 which included a goal from Ibrahimovic which was a bit of a freak goal according to Hutchison.

"I think he chipped the 'keeper from about 40 yards."

The tyranny of distance probably shortened both of their international careers, something that plagued Australian sides through the 1980s and 1990s, and there were also no official FIFA windows within the A-League.

Hutchison was restricted in how many times he could represent Malta.

"I would have missed probably six to eight games. The club didn't release you until 48 hours before a friendly game and 72 hours for an actual game. For me to leave home on the Central Coast and to get to the hotel in Malta was about 33 hours door to door.

"Some games I was never going to make it. One game I tried to get to was against Georgia in Georgia. It worked out to be about 43 hours to get there, I would have made it with an hour to spare before kick-off."

Wellington were more lenient for Muscat, but there was still a lot of travel.

"We'd travel up to 28 hours to get back to Malta. You only have a handful of days to prepare yourself and you were jetlagged.

"At times it was fun and awesome playing the big teams, but the at the same time it was quite hard on your body."

It is with a real sense of pride that Hutchison looks at his time with Malta.

"When I rang my grandma to tell her I was representing Malta, she was crying and telling me how proud she was for me to represent her country.

"It's almost on top of my list of achievements as a footballer. I say that with everything else in my career that I've done.

"To play in those stadiums and travel around the world doing something that I love doing, it was an incredible experience. Representing my grandma's and pop's home country and my grandma still being alive to watch the games was pretty surreal at times."

Muscat is also hugely proud of what it meant to his family.

"I think my parents are my number one fans, so to go back and to represent their country and to go back to visit their family while we were there as well made them happy. They just want to see me do well at anything I do. They were very pleased."

***

Buddy Farah is a Sydney based, prominent player agent with some of Australia's best known footballers on his books, but it is his career as a professional player that could almost be the script for a movie or a book of its own.

A prominent NSL player in Sydney with Marconi, Sydney-born Farah represented the Olyroos leading up to the Sydney Olympics in 2000 before being chosen for the country of his parents' birth, Lebanon, for qualifiers for the Japan/South Korea 2002 World Cup.

Farah had the chance to move to clubs in Europe and Saudi Arabia, but these moves were knocked back by coaching and transfer fee issues. Eventually he moved to Lebanon and felt the highs and lows of world football. When on tour with Lebanon, Farah and his teammates had their possessions stolen from the dressing rooms during an international. He also scored the winning goal playing away against North Korea. His club football in Lebanon saw him play in front of home crowds averaging 40,000 people and he was sponsored by Coca-Cola. But whilst there Farah also became gravely ill, he almost required an emergency liver transplant before he decided to cut all ties and head back home to Australia.

These experiences have helped forge a successful career as a player agent, giving Farah a sound understanding of the workings of the Middle East, its clubs and its players.

The first approach by Lebanon to Farah to play for the national team was something straight out of a spy movie. The offer came at the airport, with Farah in an Australian tracksuit.

"It was actually prior to me travelling for a training camp with the Olyroos in Holland. Prior to the camp I had someone approach me at the airport. It was an approach by a representative of the Lebanese FA for me to come over and represent Lebanon and not to represent Australia."

Farah did want to represent Australia, grateful for the opportunities the country had provided him and his family.

Frank Farina was Farah's coach at Marconi and when Farina was appointed Socceroos coach, Farah approached him about his chances of a Socceroos callup.

In discussions with Farina, Farah was told that unless he was playing abroad, he probably wouldn't be considered for the national team. Most of the golden generation were playing their football overseas. Farah had tried previously to get to Europe, but circumstances prevented it from happening.

"I was 19 years old and heading abroad to play at FC Copenhagen, but once I was in the Olyroos that deal was sabotaged by a club asking too much for a transfer fee, Marconi.

"I had an opportunity to go to FC Twente straight out of the Olyroos and the Olympic games. Prior to me flying over to Holland they sacked the coach. The new coach didn't want any foreigners so I was asked keep the ticket refund and that opportunity was taken from under me. I had two good cracks at two good clubs in Europe and unfortunately due to circumstances they never transpired."

When the Lebanese FA came calling the second time around, Farah was more willing to listen. Realising his chances of making the Socceroos squad were slim, he made the decision to play for The Cedars.

"It was a matter of making a decision there and then. When a door opens, you definitely have to look at what's inside that door. So I did it, it was a great experience, it was an eye opener. I could probably say I was one of the first, if not the first, to play against most of the Asian nations that Australia plays against now."

In 20 caps for Lebanon Farah scored one goal, away against North Korea. This was a game more memorable for the treatment afforded the visiting country.

"It was a moment that I will probably never forget because the week leading into the game was probably, as a football team, the worst experience you'd go through you know. We were having to cook our own breakfasts, lunch and dinners because we never trusted the cooks in the hotels. The food we were getting served, you wouldn't feed to your dog and the training pitch we were on, had goats on it!

"Everything was confiscated at the airport when we landed and was handed back to us when we left. It was something that I really couldn't believe. I mean no cameras, no phones, no computers, nothing at the time. Just fantastic."

The poor treatment of visiting countries was not limited in the region to North Korea. Farah played in Syria in a game that was abandoned at half time due to theft.

"They broke into our changerooms and stole pretty much all our stuff while we were out on the pitch playing for our country. We came into the changerooms in Syria at half time and I found that my whole bag was gone. My passport, my jewellery; at the time we were using Walkmans as our form of music, so my Walkman, my camera and my credit cards. So they had to abandon the game!"

After representing Lebanon, Farah would return to Australia to play in the NSL with Wollongong Wolves. Prior to him finishing his contract there, Nejmeh, the largest club in Lebanon which was run by the then Prime Minister's son, asked Farah to join them. Farah took the opportunity with both hands.

"It was the biggest club. It was always attracting the best players and everyone wanted to play for the club. It was almost like back in the NSL, Marconi was the club you wanted to play for. Nejmeh paid the most and they had the biggest following. They usually played in the Asian Champions League and the captain of the national team was a big icon and he played for that team.

"I played for the national team and gained the respect of the captain and he was also the captain of Nejmeh. He was the one who put in the call to me. I was back here in Wollongong, he said *'Look we would like you to consider coming to join us at the end of your playing contract at Wollongong, you'd be well looked after. We've obviously seen your qualities in the national team and we'd really like you to be part of it'*.

"So that's why I went and I was paid quite well to do so. I was a young father,

I had my first child at 21, so I also had to look at it from a family perspective and that was also the end of the NSL pretty much."

With a substantial pay rise behind him and a sponsorship with Coca-Cola, Farah was playing for Nejmeh, the largest club in Lebanon, but it was a freak illness that ended his career with both Nejmeh and Lebanon.

"I copped hepatitis at the time that made me spend nine solid days in hospital! It was actually in the lead up to a big game, a big derby match and the night before I felt ill.

"The doctors came to my hotel and ruled me out of the game. They put me into a room and pumped some injections into me. Because of a misdiagnosis those injections were triggering an inflammation of my liver. I ended up in hospital and almost had a liver transplant. Luckily enough I recovered in time to not undergo surgery.

"That led me to pretty much walk away from playing in Lebanon. Whilst I was recovering, they never fulfilled their end of the bargain by paying me my salary. When I decided to chase it up, they decided to play games which was unusual. I didn't expect it because they actually looked after me quite well when I was there. I was paid well, I was sponsored by Coca-Cola and things were on the up and then all of a sudden I got sick and they refused to fulfil their end of the bargain. When there was still an outstanding amount of my salary, I ended the relationship with the club. This also resulted in me refusing to play for the country."

These freakish experiences in the region forged the beginnings of Farah's post football career as a successful player agent.

"I went on to represent two of my former teammates who went on to the Bundesliga. I became their agent for a number of deals into China and the Middle East. I firmly believe things do happen for a reason and that experience probably defines me as a person now. It gave me a leg up in the region knowing how things operate.

"I looked after two of Lebanon's greatest legends as an agent, and I am still looking to assist some young talented players who don't get the opportunity to progress outside that league. That's a little bit of my story."

* * *

Daniel Georgievski was born in Blacktown, New South Wales to Macedonian parents and played his junior football with Marconi.

Prior to a family holiday in the Balkans, Georgievski made a highlights tape and sent it to Croatia's famous Dinamo Zagreb earning a trial.

"I did well and then they asked me to play. So it went from there."

He joined the youth setup in Zagreb as an Under 19 player.

Georgievski would begin an arduous and tough playing career in Europe with three Croatian clubs and a Romanian club. He won titles, played Champions League and Europa League before returning to Australia with Melbourne Victory and then the Newcastle Jets.

The only time anyone from Australian football approached Georgievski overseas was when he first signed for Croatian club Medimurje. They received a letter asking for a $250,000 training compensation fee for the junior clubs he played for in Sydney. Medimurje did not have the funds to pay this, and luckily for Georgievski his agent was able to talk them out of the compensation as he had never played any junior representative football.

"That was the only time they made contact. Anyone from Australia. When they wanted compensation."

From there Macedonia came calling and a 24-year old Georgievski was asked to play in World Cup and European Qualifiers. Georgievski's father suggested he hold off and see if Australia called him up for the Socceroos. However, given there had been no contact from the country of his birth previously, he threw his lot in with his heritage.

Georgievski made his debut for Macedonia at right back, playing against Russia in Moscow in a 2-0 loss.

Career highlights with the Macedonian national team included the battles with Balkan neighbours Serbia and Croatia which included a 1-0 victory at home in Skopje against the Serbs.

"There is that Balkan history with Yugoslavia so it meant a little bit more. Serbia were a very good team with players from the Premier League. Just to play against them was amazing and then to actually beat them at home was great; people don't forget that.

"We had a couple of close calls against Croatia too. We should have won at Zagreb, should have been awarded two or three penalties, but you know we are Macedonian and they are Croatian so obviously they got the benefit of the doubt in that game. We showed that we were not going to be pushed over. It is definitely worth remembering."

At the end of Georgievski's frustrating club football in Romania, he transferred to the A-League with Melbourne Victory and, being Australian-born, he was not considered a foreign or visa player. He was then called back to Macedonia, who were scheduled to play a friendly against Australia.

"It was funny because I was living in Australia when we played them. I'd only been back for four or five months. I think Australia had just beaten Germany. They were on a bit of a high.

"When the national anthems came up it was quite funny because I knew both of them. I was just having a bit of a grin and biting my tongue a little bit when the Australian one was on.

"It was good, I didn't know most of the Aussie players and they didn't know me, but with me speaking in an Australian accent they were like *"Who is this bloke?"*. For them too it was a bit of a laugh."

The 0-0 draw with Australia was to be Georgievski's 22nd and final cap for

Macedonia. Swapping shirts at the end of the game he sought out an Aussie he had played against previously in Spain.

"I changed shirts with [Oliver] Bozanic. I had met him 18 months prior in a pre-season tournament, he was playing for a Swiss team and we were playing against him. I knew the captain of his team and he had told me that they had an Australian player there. So that's where I first met Oli and we had a bit of a chat.

"A few months later he came to Melbourne Victory and we became teammates.

"A funny little thing that happens in the wonderful world of football."

10
Lost Socceroos Short Stories

Lost Socceroos conjures up all kinds of potential opportunities and many stories. I am sure I have only written a small amount. There are plenty more that are worth exploring, perhaps in a follow up book, here are a few.

In 1947 **Ken Grieves** was a cricketer of some note who moved to England aged 22. Having played nine games of Sheffield Shield cricket with New South Wales, Grieves went to Rawtenstall Cricket Club in the Lancashire league as the overseas professional. He was a last-minute replacement for Australian superstar Keith Miller. Before his cricket career began, he was lining up as a goalkeeper for Bury in a Lancashire Cup tie against Liverpool. Grieves became an accomplished player at two sports, spending his winters as goalkeeper for Wigan Athletic, Stockport County and Bolton Wanderers. He even featured on the cover of the Football Association Yearbook of 1956-57. In cricket he played 452 games for Lancashire and holds the record for the most catches, suggesting a safe pair of hands, something he required in playing both sports at the highest level possible in the north of England. Grieves never returned to Australia, and the Socceroos didn't pick an overseas based player until Jim Patikas in 1988.

Moving from Greece to Melbourne after World War II, **Georgios Samaras** helped establish the South Melbourne Hellas Football Club in 1952. They would become one of the most famous and storied clubs in Australian football. Up until 2018, South Melbourne have produced more Socceroos than any other club. Samaras would move back to Greece with his family, including his Melbourne born son Ioannis (John) who was 13 at the time. Between 1986 and 1990, the Melbourne born John would play 16 times for Greece. John even played a one game cameo for South Melbourne in 1987, coming off the bench to score a goal in wet conditions. John's son born in 1985, also called Georgios, would have an even more storied career. Georgios played for famous clubs such as Manchester City and Celtic. He would also play 81 times for Greece as a winger and striker. There was constant speculation towards the end of his career that he would join the A-League, able to play as a non-visa player due to his Australian heritage. It never happened.

David Oldfield was a six-foot tall midfielder who played over 600 games in the United Kingdom. He is famous in the blue half of Manchester after scoring two goals for City in a famous 5-1 derby win over Manchester United at Maine Road in 1989. That result put the elite coaching career of United's Alex Ferguson in serious jeopardy. Oldfield was born in Perth, Western Australia, but appears never to have been approached by the management of the Socceroos.

Ersan Gulum was born in Melbourne to Turkish parents. He started his football with Hume City. He was recruited to Manisaspor in the Turkish Super League after they saw him playing for a touring Australian Schoolboys team in the United Kingdom. Gulum was part of the Olyroos team that tried to qualify for the 2008 Beijing Olympics, playing twice for the green and gold. Despite playing high level football in Turkey, Gulum was continually frustrated with his lack of opportunities with the senior Socceroos. Holger Osieck selected him in a preliminary squad of 50 for the 2011 Asian Cup, and when he failed to make the final 23, he chose to change his allegiance to Turkey. Turkey at the time were being coached by former Socceroos saviour Guus Hiddink. Osieck accused Hiddink of stockpiling talent and not selecting his national team on any form or merit. Speaking to AAP at the time Osieck said:

"Maybe it is a little bit of a rush because they do not want to lose another player because they missed out on a couple of Turks who grew up in Europe and Germany and they got a lot of stick for that. I think no matter what quality a player offers ... it is like being collectors that collect players for the sake of collecting. Whether they can really use the players, in respect of the team and where they fit with the spine of the team ... I don't think they have a real plan."

Playing 94 times for Besiktas, Gulum then earned seven caps for Turkey between 2013 and 2015. His Australian passport helped when he transferred on a big money deal to the Chinese Super League with Hebei China Fortune. Gulum was then loaned out to Adelaide United for the 2017-18 A League season.

Gethin Wynne Jones sounds Welsh. That's because he is Welsh. Born to Welsh parents, he grew up in Wales and joined Everton's Academy as a 12-year old. He went on to represent Wales, and captain them at Under 17, Under 19 and Under 21 level. He left Everton for League One outfit Fleetwood Town and was then approached by Australia to join its Under 23 side. How can this be? Gethin was born in Perth, Western Australia and has dual eligibility. At this stage of his career he has not represented either Wales or Australia at senior national level.

Similar to Christian Vieri, South Korea's **Ki Sung-Yong** spent four of his most formative years playing football and learning the game in Australia. As a 12-year old, he joined Brisbane's John Paul College as part of their Sports Academy. He was known then by the Anglicised name 'David'. At 16 his talent saw him weigh up two professional opportunities, one with FC Seoul back in South Korea and one with the Brisbane Roar

Youth setup. He chose to return to South Korea and his football career never looked back. He has played club football in the UK with Celtic, Swansea, Sunderland and Newcastle United. He credits his time in Australia as helping him settle into English-speaking countries. The national team career of Ki Sung-Yong is even more impressive. He has been capped over 100 times, going to the 2010, 2014 and 2018 World Cups, the 2018 edition as captain, as well as the London Olympics in 2012. He is most likely to be remembered in Australia for the 2015 Asian Cup final where he provided the assist for South Korea to equalise, forcing extra time.

Iain Ramsay was born in Perth, Western Australia to a Scottish father and a Filipino mother. After trying his football luck in Scotland, Iain came back to Australia and played 125 A-League games with Sydney FC, Adelaide United and Melbourne City. In 2015 Ramsay left Australia to begin an Asian football adventure which would see him play in Iran, the Philippines, Malaysia and Thailand. Ramsay was also called into the Philippines squad in 2015 for their World Cup Qualifiers, making history as three years later he helped them qualify for their first ever major tournament, the 2019 Asian Cup. The Filipinos made a concerted effort to find players of heritage for their football squad. Their team is now quite diverse and includes many Europeans as well as Ramsay. Coached by the famous Swede Sven Goran Eriksson they unfortunately lost all of their group games at the Asian Cup. They did have some success with their first goal in a major competition, German born Stephan Schrock scoring against Kyrgyzstan.

Leeds United have always had a love/hate relationship with Australia and Australian footballers. They have loved our players, not only the eight Socceroos mentioned in the Tony Dorigo chapter, but also Australians Shane Cansdell-Sheriff, Danny Milosevic, Shane Lowry, Sasa Ilic and Jamie McMaster. Work permit issues denied them Ned Zelic and Brett Emerton as well. They have hated the distance to Australia when having to release players such as Kewell and Viduka to Socceroos camps and games. Seeing this as weakening their side.

Jamie McMaster was born in Sydney and joined Leeds United youth academy as a teenager, plucked from the same high school as Harry Kewell. Keen to not have another first teamer missing due to international duties like they had with Kewell, McMaster was encouraged by Leeds United to play for England. He did at Under 18 and Under 20 level, despite his parents being Scottish. McMaster's career never really took off in the UK. He played 11 times for Leeds and was loaned to several lower division sides over the years. McMaster eventually returned to Australia and the A-League with Central Coast Mariners. Whilst at Central Coast he made a request to FIFA to be eligible for Australia again, telling The World Game in 2006 of his reasons:

"It was nothing to do with turning my back (on Australia). I just decided on (England). And Leeds, as a big, massive club, didn't want me to travel back and forth to Australia at such a young age. I learnt so much from it... and I don't hide the fact that I played for

England. But I'm Australian. And I'm Australian through and through now."

McMaster did not go on to represent the Socceroos.

The Socceroos played their first national game in 1922. Pre-1922 we could call all of our great footballers lost Socceroos. There is one Australian trailblazer of the time that we should take a closer look at, **James 'Jimmy' Jackson.** Jackson was born in Scotland but moved to Australia at the age of two, growing up in the football mad area of Newcastle, New South Wales. He played senior football for the famous Australian clubs of the area, Hamilton Athletic and then Adamstown Rosebud when still a teenager.

At 18 years of age, Jackson returned to Scotland and would play for Rangers. Jackson would also play in England with Newcastle United, Arsenal and West Ham, all prior to World War I. His two sons James and Archie, who were born in England, would also have great footballing careers. James played over 200 games for Liverpool, and Archie played for Sunderland and Tranmere Rovers. The Jackson family had a big connection with Australia with Jimmy's nephew Archie Jackson, born in Scotland but Australian raised, becoming a teenage cricket sensation.

Archie Jackson played first grade cricket at 15, played for New South Wales at 17 and then at 19 scored 164 on test debut for Australia. He became the youngest person to score a test century. Tragically, Archie died of tuberculosis aged only 23.

Graeme Rutjes is a defender who played with Excelsior in the Netherlands before playing over 300 games in Belgium with K.V.Mechelen and Anderlecht. Graeme went on to earn 13 caps with the Netherlands, including being part of their World Cup squad at Italia '90. Rutjes was born in Sydney.

The Melbourne-born Greek **Avraam Papadopoulos** carved out a serviceable career in Europe at Greek clubs Aris and Olympiakos and as well as earning 37 caps with Greece. His time with the Greek national team included the 2010 World Cup in South Africa. Holding an Australian passport, Avraam was able to play in China with Shanghai Shenhua and it also led to his return to Australia in the A-League with Brisbane Roar, playing as an Australian in that squad.

When asked of the chances of Heart of Midlothian's centre back **John Souttar** being picked for Scotland, manager Craig Levein said *"He's got an Aussie granny!"*. In a backhanded way of alerting the Scots to Souttar's dual eligibility, Levein stated he wasn't trying to influence the selectors, he just wanted to alert them.

It may have worked for Scotland and Hearts, as John Souttar was capped by Scotland in 2018. It may also have assisted the Socceroos in another way. John's younger brother **Harry Souttar** was on the books at Stoke City in England and despite playing Under 17 and Under 19 for Scotland, was picked in Graham Arnold's Under 23 Olyroos squad and played in Olympic qualifiers 2019, as well as for the Socceroos in an international friendly against Korea in the same year.

Playing in the domestic competitions of the NSL or the A-League should be putting you in the 'shop window' for Australian selection. History tells us some coaches of the Socceroos would always prefer those playing overseas, and the following can count themselves unlucky that they missed out for various reasons. The players with the most national games without an international cap for the Socceroos are:

- 389 **David Barrett** – Sydney Olympic, Sydney United, Parramatta Power
- 377 **Gary Phillips** – Sydney Olympic, Brisbane Strikers
- 353 **Danny Wright** – Brisbane Lions, South Melbourne, Brisbane Strikers
- 330 **Robert Stanton** – Sydney United, Marconi, Wollongong
- 326* **Liam Reddy** – Parramatta Power, Sydney United, Newcastle Jets, Brisbane Roar, Wellington Phoenix, Sydney FC, Central Coast Mariners, Western Sydney Wanderers, Perth Glory
- 321 **Andrew Harper** – Sydney City, Sydney Olympic, St George, Brisbane Strikers, Newcastle Breakers, Newcastle United
- 310 **John Gibson** – Blacktown City, APIA Leichardt, Adelaide City, West Adelaide, Parramatta Power, Marconi

still playing at time of print

Australia played many club teams touring from overseas and this led to a number of players playing for the Socceroos in games that were not considered full internationals. 322 footballers have represented Australia in B-internationals.

Migrating from Scotland to Melbourne, **Johnny Johnstone** played 26 times for the Socceroos without ever playing a full international and Ipswich's **Spencer Kitching** played 21 games, could they be considered lost Socceroos? It's worth reading Andrew Howe's *Encyclopedia of Socceroos* for more on these many and varied players.

Christian Vieri (Italy) and Max Vieri (Australia) featured in an earlier chapter. They are one of three sets of brothers who have had siblings represent another country as well as Australia.

Socceroo Tim Cahill's brother Chris was part of Samoa's World Cup qualifying campaign in 2010 earning three caps in 2007.

Thomas Deng debuted for the Socceroos in 2018, his older brother Peter having represented South Sudan once in 2016.

What might have been with some of the great code hoppers within Australian sports? Some standout junior football players who went on to excel at other sports include Australian Rules goal kicking sensation Peter McKenna of Collingwood and Rugby League great, Newcastle's Andrew Johns. The Sydney Swans Adam Goodes and Australian cricket's Waugh twins Stephen and Mark are others.

Adam Goodes played junior football in South Australia before moving to Victoria when he was 14. On arrival they went to the local football club to sign up, but they did not have a junior team and the senior game was quite spiteful at the time.

At the same time across the road the Merebin Under 14 Australian Rules team was playing, Goodes appeared to be a lot taller than those players and his mother suggested he play that instead. Goodes was lost to the world game and would go on to an incredible career in the Australian Football League, winning the premiership twice, be the club games record holder for the Sydney Swans as well as win the Brownlow Medal (best player in the competition) twice, playing in different positions each time!

Steve and Mark Waugh were prodigiously talented at any sport they turned to. Early on they became state representatives in both cricket and football. Socceroo and media legend Johnny Warren even wrote about Steve Waugh back in 1983 in the *Sydney Morning Herald* when he was covering a high school tournament:

"I have not seen a better goal this year than the one scored by East Hills High School's Stephen Waugh in the Commonwealth Bank Cup at Mt Druitt Town Soccer Centre last Wednesday evening. It was a goal of which the legendary Franz Beckenbauer would have been proud."

The Waugh's would end up playing for NSL club Sydney Croatia, before their cricket career took over and they were forced to give football away.

Steve Waugh would captain Australia, playing 168 tests and winning the World Cup in 1987 and 1999 as captain. Mark would play 128 tests and would dominate the World Cup of 1996 before being part of the winning team in 1999. Another what might have been for Australia.

Mark Bresciano played 84 times for the Socceroos, including three World Cups and being part of the Asian Cup triumph of 2015. Being of Italian heritage his senior football career was mainly in the Serie A playing with clubs such as Empoli, Parma, Palermo and Lazio.

Italian great **Giovanni Trapattoni** has a most impressive managerial CV which includes Juventus, AC Milan and Bayern Munich. He was also the Italian manager between 2000 and 2004. In 2002 Trapattoni approached Bresciano about his eligibility for the Italian side, not knowing that he was a Socceroo. Luckily for Australia he had already been capped.

Mark Robertson played in Australia with Marconi, Wollongong, Sydney FC and Perth Glory in between stints in England and Scotland, earning a Socceroos cap in 2001 against the Solomon Islands. His father **Alex Robertson** also played for Australia.

Given the nature of world football and of the world, Mark had a son, **Alexander**, with his Peruvian partner in Scotland. Alexander was raised in Perth and now also qualifies for England as he forms part of Manchester City's junior Academy. Four countries can all now lay claim to him if he is good enough.

Former Socceroo captain **Lucas Neill**'s son has recently joined Liverpool's Academy. With an English mother, he will also have options if he's good enough.

OUR LOST SOCCEROOS

This is only the beginning. With our global village getting smaller and smaller, more and more players will have the choice of countries and allegiances, let's hope that more often than not they choose the Socceroos.

Acknowledgements

Thank you to the following people for their time providing interviews, feedback, referrals, translations, introductions, suggestions, information, answers, encouragement, reviews and beds to sleep on.

Adam Howard, Andrew Durante, Andrew Howe, Ange Postecoglou, Ante Milicic, Attilio Labbozetta, Bonita Mersiades, Buddy Farah, Chris Woolridge, Craig Johnston, Daniel Garb, Daniel Georgievski, Dominic Bossi, Drac Matijevic, Eileen Perkins, Elia Santoro, Frank Farina, George Negus, Graham Fulton, Goran Drapac, Dr Gordon Briscoe, Graham Fulton, Ivan Ergic, Joe Gorman, Joey Didulica, John Didulica, John Hutchison, John Maynard, John Moriarty, Lucas Gillard, Manny Muscat, Matthew Hall, Michael Lynch, Nataly Matijevic, Ned Zelic, Patrick Skene, Paul Mavroudis, Paul Okon, Rachel Perkins, Ron Smith, Roy Hay, Sasa Ilic, Shane Smeltz, Steve O'Connor, Stuart Donald, Stuart Downey, Tony Dorigo, Tony Labbozetta, Tracylee Tombides, Vesna Drapac, Zlatko Drapac.

Plus the following great assistance from football clubs who responded to my interview requests: Newcastle Jets, Wellington Phoenix, Seattle Sounders, Green Gully and Leeds United.

My former work colleagues Rodrigo Rodriguez (Michael Petrucelli), Simon Crivelli and Simon Barton, Paul from Burnley Barber Shop and Neil Edwards - great to reconnect and talk soccer after 20 years.

The sporting teams and teammates of my past: Vancouver Meralomas, Richmond City, Taringa Rovers, Eastlake, Dirk Digglers, St Josephs, Buffalo Celtics, St Johns-Bluebirds, Canberra Cockies, the Dads that took on the Thornbury United coaches and most importantly Ferntree Gully.

A special shout out to Eric, Paul and John from *Punting for Brazil* and then Russia and now Qatar. We started gambling once a week to earn enough money to heard to Brazil in 2014. We earned enough money to go to Phillip Island instead. We stayed at my parents' holiday home. For free.

My beautiful wife Sophie for letting me follow a passion and my wonderful children Henry and Ivy. I love you all and always aim to make you proud.

Finally Jordan Caridi. When I floated the book idea you helped provide feedback, encouragement, translations and with a memory like a steel trap, always gave some guidance. I value our friendship mate and appreciate your support.

About Jason Goldsmith

Jason Goldsmith grew up in Ferntree Gully in the eastern suburbs of Melbourne, Australia. A massive sports fan, he was fed a diet of cricket in the summer (Ferntree Gully Cricket Club) and Aussie rules in the winter (Collingwood). His best mate from primary school, Jordan Caridi, was of Italian heritage and slowly introduced him to the world game.

Jason's love for Australian football began with Ned Zelic in the 'spew shirt' taking the Olyroos to the Barcelona Olympics in 1992 and then intensified with Maradona mania, as Diego and Argentina took on the Socceroos in the final playoff for the 1994 World Cup.

His best moment as a player was scoring in the Dads v Coaches win at a Thornbury United Junior Football clinic for his son.

His best moment as a fan, convincing his wife to honeymoon in South Africa in 2010, taking in all the Socceroos group games.

He lives in the inner north of Melbourne with his wife Sophie, children Henry and Ivy.

A collector of Australian soccer/football books and a self-described amateur historian, Jason saw a gap in some Australian stories that needed to be told and went about putting together *Surfing for England*, all about the Lost Socceroos. He hopes this is the first book of many.

Other books by Fair Play Publishing

Encyclopedia of Matildas by Andrew Howe and Greg Werner

Chronicles of Australian Soccer, 1859-1949 by Peter Kunz

'If I started to cry, I wouldn't stop' by Matthew Hall

Support Your Local League by Antony Sutton

Playing for Australia – the First Socceroos, Asia and World Football by Trevor Thompson

World Cup Chronicles – 31 Days that Rocked Brazil by Jorge Knijnik

Encyclopedia of Socceroos by Andrew Howe

From Popcorn Press

The Time of My Football Life by David Picken

Introducing Jarrod Black and *Jarrod Black – Hospital Pass* by Texi Smith

From Powderhouse Press (USA)

Whatever It Takes – the Inside Story of the FIFA Way by Bonita Mersiades

www.fairplaypublishing.com.au

www.ingramcontent.com/pod-product-compliance
Lightning Source LLC
Chambersburg PA
CBHW042128100526
44587CB00026B/4216